THE HOUR IS NOW

THE HOUR IS NOW

MAITY SCHRECENGOST

XULON PRESS

Xulon Press
2301 Lucien Way #415
Maitland, FL 32751
407.339.4217
www.xulonpress.com

© 2019 by Maity Schrecengost

All rights reserved solely by the author. The author guarantees all contents are original and do not infringe upon the legal rights of any other person or work. No part of this book may be reproduced in any form without the permission of the author. The views expressed in this book are not necessarily those of the publisher.

Unless otherwise indicated, Scripture quotations taken from the King James Version (KJV). Copyright © 1972 by Thomas Nelson, Inc. Used by permission. All rights reserved.

Printed in the United States of America.

ISBN-13: 978-1-5456-7531-1

DEDICATION

This book is dedicated to the glory of God and to all who see in Jesus Christ the complete fulfillment of Biblical Messianic prophecies.

ACKNOWLEDGMENTS

No one writes a book alone. I want to offer thanks to the many people who helped and encouraged me in the process of creating **The Hour Is Now**:

- the Holy Spirit who planted the germ of the idea for the book in my heart and inspired the writing of it;

- the many fine people at Xulon Press who guided me in making the book a reality;

- Donna Vermillion who gave me Tobias' name;

- Bette Troike who, unknowingly, confirmed the title, and, last but by no means least,

- Tom, my husband, best friend, and relentless critic who read – and read – and reread the manuscript.

To each of you I offer a huge heartfelt, "Thank you!"

Dear Reader,

I invite you to travel back in time with me, over 2000 years, to meet Tobias and his family, and to experience life as Tobias knew it in Biblical times when Jesus walked among men.

Many writings about Jesus for young readers are told as Bible stories or are told through the eyes of grown-ups. I want you to see Jesus through the eyes of a young boy who might have lived in a time and place far removed from your modern life, in the little village of Capernaum in Galilee.

Try to imagine being a Jewish boy living with his family in Capernaum when Jesus walked the paths of this fishing village. Can you see in your mind the rocky shore of the Sea of Galilee? Can you picture yourself climbing mountains or crossing barren deserts in Israel? Can you imagine walking the streets of Jerusalem or seeing Herod's magnificent Temple? **The Hour Is Now** will take you to these places - and many more!

Tobias and his family are, of course, not real people, and their experiences took place only in my imagination. But Jesus, his words, teachings and the events surrounding his life are true as recorded in Scripture. For the sake of story, I have sometimes put words in the mouths of historical Biblical characters as I have imagined they would have spoken them, but I have always tried to remain true to the meaning of scripture.

I have not tried to record the events in strict chronological order. Even the gospel writers do not always agree on exactly when events took place! At the end of this book, you will find a listing of "Events in the Life of Jesus" in the order in which they occur in **The Hour Is Now** with references to Scripture passages in the Gospels where they may be found.

I hope that as you walk with Tobias, you will be able to enter into his life as he lived it in 30 AD. More than that, I hope you will come to recognize Jesus as the promised Messiah, as Tobias did, and will welcome Him into your heart.

Maity Schrecengost

Where Jesus Walked

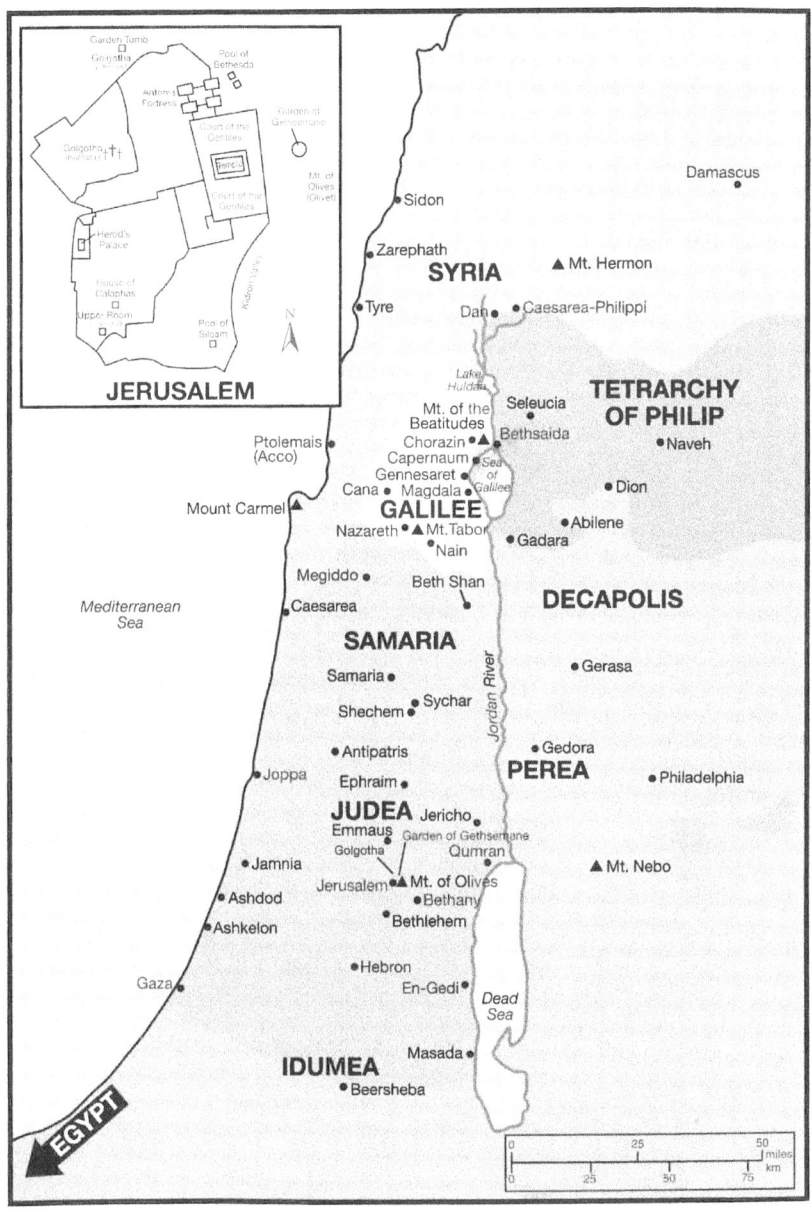

Holy Land Map used by permission of Rose Publishing,
Rose Book of Bible Charts, Maps, & Time Lines,
10th Anniversary, Expanded Edition

TABLE OF CONTENTS

Dedication v
Acknowledgments vii
Chapter 1 - A Story 1
Chapter 2 - A Wedding 5
Chapter 3 - A Rumor 13
Chapter 4 - A Mystery 17
Chapter 5 - A Healing 20
Chapter 6 - A Big Question 23
Chapter 7 - An Offering 26
Chapter 8 - A Miracle 30
Chapter 9 - A Lesson 33
Chapter 10 - A Threat 35
Chapter 11 - A Rule Breaker 38
Chapter 12 - A Raising 42
Chapter 13 - A Question 46
Chapter 14 - A Touch 49
Chapter 15 - A Journey 52
Chapter 16 - A Celebration 55
Chapter 17 - A Confession 58
Chapter 18 - An Anointing 62
Chapter 19 - A Sacrifice 65
Chapter 20 - A Meal 68
Chapter 21 - An Arrest 70
Chapter 22 - A Trial 73
Chapter 23 - A Crucifixion 75
Chapter 24 - A Resurrection 79
Epilogue - A Beginning 83
Events in the Life of Jesus as related in
The Hour Is Now with a Scripture Reference 85

Chapter 1

A Story

Tobias and Rachel sat cross-legged on woven mats placed on the packed clay floor in front of their Grandfather. The old man's eyes twinkled as he tugged at his beard while shifting to a more comfortable position. The children fastened their eyes on him, waiting for him to speak. Rachel's black curls bobbed when she bounced impatiently saying, "Now, Grandfather. Now! Tell us a story now!"

Tobias poked her with his elbow. "Sit still, Rachel. Grandfather will begin when he's ready."

Grandfather looked lovingly at the children. God had blessed him with a full quiver of grandchildren, but these two – Tobias, ten years old and Rachel seven – his daughter's children, had a special place in his heart.

A smile tugged at his lips as he tried to speak sternly, "Settle down now, you two. Get ready to listen. The story I will tell today is an old one; it took place many years ago."

"How long ago was it?" Rachel questioned eagerly. "Before you were even born?"

"Oh, my, yes. It was very long before I was born. It happened nearly 1000 years ago during the time when kings ruled Israel. But this story is not about a king, it's about a prophet named Elisha."

"You mean Elijah, Grandfather?" Tobias questioned.

"No, Grandson. Not Eli*jah*, Eli*sha*. But Elijah does have a part in the story, too. You see, one day when the prophet

Elijah went walking, he saw Elisha plowing his father's field. As Elijah passed by, he cast his mantle, his cloak, upon Elisha. Now Elisha knew that meant he was to follow the older man, so he left the twelve yoke of oxen and ran after Elijah crying out, 'Let me kiss my mother and father. Then I will follow you.' Elijah gave his permission. After young Elisha said good-bye to his parents, he went with Elijah."

Tobias interrupted. "If Elisha's father had twelve yoke of oxen, he must have been very rich."

"He was, but that didn't keep Elisha from being willing to leave his father's wealth behind to go with Elijah. You see, Elisha knew God had a calling on his life. During the years he spent with Elijah, he learned from him the ways of a prophet. Later, Elisha himself took Elijah's place as chief prophet. He served well and even did miracles. One of the miracles is what this story is about."

"Tell us about it, Grandfather," Rachel said impatiently.

"All right, all right, little one," Grandfather went on. "The story goes like this. One time in his travels, the prophet Elisha went to a village called Shunem. A very wealthy woman lived there and she invited him to come in and eat. After that, every time Elisha passed by Shunem, he stopped at her house. Because she knew Elisha was a man of God, the Shunamite woman convinced her husband to build a little room for him. They put a bed, a table, a stool and a candlestick in a small upstairs chamber. That little room became known as the prophet's chamber."

"A room all to himself," Tobias said, rolling his eyes. "I'd love that!"

"Elisha did, too. He was so grateful for their kindness, he sent his servant, Gehazi, to ask the woman what he could do for her in return. The woman told Gehazi she had everything she wanted except one thing. She said she had no child and that she and her husband were now too old to have children.

When Gehazi told Elisha what the woman said, Elisha asked Gehazi to tell her to come and stand in the doorway of the prophet's chamber. As she stood there, Elisha told her that in a year's time she would hold her baby son in her arms.

And it came to pass just as Elisha said."

"But, Grandfather," Rachel asked, "how did Elisha know the woman would have a baby?"

Grandfather rumpled Rachel's curls as he explained. "He knew because God told him, Rachel. That's what prophets do; they hear from God and tell people what they hear."

"It must be wonderful to be a prophet and hear from God," Tobias mused.

"Yes," Grandfather went on, "but the story doesn't end there. The boy grew and one day the lad went out into the field where his father was reaping. It was very hot and after a time the boy said, 'My head, my head.' His father told a servant to take the boy to his mother. The servant carried the boy and laid him in the mother's arms. She held him on her lap until noon. Then the boy died."

"Grandfather, that's not a happy ending!" Rachel wailed.

"It's not the ending, Rachel! The story isn't finished. The woman carried her dead son to the prophet's chamber and laid him on Elisha's bed. Then she told her servants to saddle an ass so she could ride out to find the man of God.

When Elisha saw her coming toward him in the distance, he sent Gehazi to meet her. Gehazi ran back to Elisha with the sad news that the boy was dead. Elisha told him to go on ahead to Shunem. He was to take Elisha's staff and lay it on the boy's face. Elisha said that he and the boy's mother would follow.

Gehazi did as he was told, but it was no use. The boy didn't speak or even seem to hear when Gehazi spoke to him. So Gehazi hurried back to meet the prophet and the boy's mother on their way to Shunem to tell them the boy had not awakened.

When Elisha and the boy's mother arrived at the prophet's chamber, Elisha went in, shut the door and prayed. Then he laid himself upon the dead child as he remembered Elijah once had done. As he stretched himself upon the boy's dead body, he felt the boy's skin begin to grow warm.

Elisha walked back and forth in the house. Then he returned to the chamber and again stretched himself on the boy. Suddenly, the boy sneezed seven times and opened his eyes. He was alive!"

Rachel clapped her hands in delight. "That's a wonderful story, Grandfather. The little boy came back to life!"

"He was dead - and then he was alive. How could it be possible, Grandfather?" questioned Tobias.

Grandfather began to say, "With God all things are possible ..." when he was interrupted by a bellow from below.

"What's going on up there?" the children's father called. "Are you filling the children's heads with nonsense? We are not like some Pharisees who believe in angels, life after death and other such foolishness. We have more sense than to believe such tales, even if they are written in the Torah. Tobias, Rachel, come down here immediately!"

A shadow darkened Grandfather's face before he said to them, "Go now, children. Obey your father."

Chapter 2

A WEDDING

Early the next day, sounds of animals stirring in the lower part of the house broke the morning's silence. The children peered over the side of the parapet edging the flat stone roof to prevent falls from the flat stone roof. Their father was supervising the loading of a wagon in the courtyard below.

Grabbing handfuls of dates from a clay bowl, Tobias and Rachel hurried down the outer stone staircase leading to the courtyard just as final bundles of fabric were being laid carefully in the wagon.

"Stand aside children. Don't get in the way now," Father barked as a servant led donkeys from the stable room.

"Where are you taking cloth today, Father?" Tobias asked.

In a gentler voice, Father answered, "To Cana, to deliver the fabrics to merchants."

Cana! Tobias loved the Cana marketplace bustling with activity. And the trip south along the coast of the Sea of Galilee from Capernaum to the village of Magdala, then west on country roads promised new sights and maybe even adventures.

"Please, Father, may I come with you?" Tobias asked hopefully.

Father looked gravely at his eager son. "I suppose," he said, "it's not too soon for you to begin to learn the ways of a merchant. Yes, son, you may come."

"May I come, too?" Rachel begged.

"Aw, Rachel," Tobias grumbled. "You're too little! Why do you always want to tag-along?"

"Because I want to see the marketplace, and the shops, and all the excitement," she coaxed. "I won't get in the way, I promise."

Who could resist such wide-eyed pleading? Not Father!

To Tobias' disgust, he gave in. "All right, Rachel. You may come along." Then he made things worse by adding, "Tobias, I'm making you responsible for your sister. Keep an eye on her at all times. Don't let her out of your sight."

Knowing argument could result in missing the trip altogether, Tobias muttered through tight lips, "Yes, Father, I'll watch out for her."

Miriam, hearing the commotion below, listened to the conversation from the rooftop. She called to her children. "Come up here, you two. Get something to eat along the way."

The children's sandals clattered on the stones as they climbed the side stairs, pausing only long enough at the doorpost to touch the mezuzah holding the sacred words of the Shema:

> *"Hear, O Israel, The Lord our God is one Lord. And thou shalt love the Lord thy God with all thine heart, and with all thy soul, and with all thy might."*

Father was very strict about the commandment to teach his children these words and to write them upon the posts of his house. As Tobias fingered the mezuzah, he was glad that his name, Tobias, meant *Yahweh is good*.

Placing packets of dried fish, small loaves of bread and chunks of goat cheese in their hands, Miriam smiled lovingly at her children as she said, "Now be good, obey your father, and stay out of trouble!" Truth to tell, she wasn't too worried about her serious son, Tobias, but she wasn't at all sure about impulsive Rachel. Tucking a stray curl behind Rachel's ear, she warned, "Rachel, stay close to your brother, you hear?"

Already pulling away to run for the stairs, Rachel called over her shoulder, "I will, Mama" and tripping lightly down the staircase she disappeared from sight. Tobias followed more slowly. Miriam's heart ached for Tobias as she watched him limping behind his sister.

With the wagon fully loaded, Father boosted Tobias over the side and lifted Rachel in to sit beside him on top of piles of fabric. The coverings protecting the fabric scratched their bare legs, but they were too excited to mind. Father climbed into the driver's seat, and they were on their way. The adventure had begun!

Before long the children caught glimpses of the Sea of Galilee through the trees. Sunlight sparkled on the still water. Fishing boats dotted the surface of the sea. The warm sun on their backs made the water seem even more inviting. They wished Father would stop the wagon and let them wade along the edges of the water a little while. But they knew better than to annoy him with what, to him, might seem to be a silly request.

At the town of Magdala, the westward path turned up through a rift in the mountains called the Valley of the Doves, leaving the sea below and behind them. High above them on a plateau towered an extinct volcano. The path through the valley was narrow, steep … and dangerous. Rachel slipped her hand into Tobias' hand and for once he didn't pull away. Both children's eyes were round as they stretched their necks to spot caves in the sheer cliffs on both sides of the path.

"Tobias," Rachel whispered. "Could there be robbers hiding in the caves?"

"Yes," Tobias answered, "and highwaymen, too. But don't worry, Father will take care of us," he said, with much more confidence than he felt.

Exciting as it was to think of the possibilities of robbers and highwaymen, both children were happy to reach the village of Arbela. Here the way turned west again. Now the path was easier. Near Arbela it wound through fields of wheat. Later it curved through mountainous regions, often with few trees to provide shade.

From time to time, as Tobias and Rachel enjoyed eating their lunches, they waved to travelers making their way from village to village. Once, when the wagon bumped over rocks on the dusty road, Tobias and Rachel giggled and bounced up and down in rhythm with the jostling of the wagon. '"Calm down, you two," Father called to them. "We're nearing the village."

Tobias and Rachel rose up on their knees for a better view as the wagon lumbered through the Cana village gates. But to their surprise and disappointment, the marketplace was nearly empty.

"Father!" shouted Tobias. "Where are all the people?"

"Who knows? Maybe there's something special going on in the village today. There may be a wedding, or a funeral. Never mind. The merchants I need to see will be here. They know I'm coming. Yes, there they are just ahead."

He brought the wagon to a halt in the marketplace, and said, "No need for you to go with me, Tobias. You two may look around a little on your own while I take care of business, but don't wander too far off. And be back here when the sun begins to drop behind those trees," he said, pointing to a row of palms.

Tobias and Rachel clambered out of the wagon eager to explore.

"Tobias," Rachel asked. "Do you hear music?"

"Yes. It sounds like it's coming from over there," he replied looking toward several side streets. "Let's follow the sound."

The music grew louder as joyful sounds led them through winding cobblestone streets to a large house. People singing, clapping and even dancing filled the courtyard. When Rachel saw a white huppah, a wedding canopy, glistening in the sun, she clapped her own hands and said, "Look, Tobias! A wedding! Come on. Let's go in."

Tobias tugged on her tunic to hold her back. "Don't be silly. We can't go in there!"

"Why can't we?" Rachel demanded.

"We haven't been invited. That's why."

"So? No one will know we weren't invited. We can just slip in and mix in with everyone else. We won't even be noticed."

"We most certainly would be noticed," Tobias said, wrinkling his sun-browned brow. "Look at the guests; don't you see what they're wearing?"

For the first time; Rachel realized that every guest wore a garment made of the same kind of fabric. "Oh! Why is everyone dressed alike?"

"It's a wedding feast! Father told me that if the groom has lots of money, he sends fabric to each invited guest to make their wedding clothes. If anyone comes dressed in something different, they're turned away. That's why we can't sneak in."

Rachel stamped her foot. "Well, then, I'm just going to go right up there and watch from the courtyard gate."

"No, you are not! You listen to me." Tobias thought for a moment. Then he said, "See that low wall alongside the courtyard, partly hidden by olive trees? We can climb up on the wall to watch and maybe no-one will see us. Come on!"

Tobias gave Rachel a leg up to an even spot on the stone wall and then struggled up to perch beside her. A careful observer might have spied two young faces and four bright eyes peering through silver-gray foliage.

Suddenly Tobias nudged Rachel and said, "Look, Rachel! There's that man everyone's been talking about. There's a woman with him and some of his followers. I think one of them is Simon Peter, and one is Peter's brother, Andrew. They are fishermen from Capernaum."

"I see him. But why are people talking about him?"

"His name is Jesus. His followers call him Master."

"Where did he come from?"

"People say he was born in Bethlehem, but grew up in Nazareth. Now he lives in Capernaum. He's a cousin of John the Baptizer."

"You mean the man who lives in the wilderness and wears camel's skin and goat's hair?"

"Yes."

"Why does he wear such funny clothes?"

"He dresses that way because he's a Nazarite."

"What's a Nazarite, Tobias?"

Tobias snapped impatiently, "A Nazarite is a man who takes a vow to never drink wine, cut his hair, touch the dead, or eat unclean food." Then, feeling bad that he had growled at Rachel, he went on. "John the Baptist goes around telling people to repent and be baptized."

"What's repent?"

"It means to be sorry for doing wrong things. Rachel, you ask too many questions! Now, be quiet! Jesus and the woman he's with are coming this way."

As the couple neared the children's hiding place among the leaves, Tobias and Rachel leaned forward straining to hear what they were saying. They heard the woman say, "Jesus, they have no wine."

Jesus replied, "Woman, what have I to do with you? My hour is not yet come." Words Tobias would think about often in the days to come.

Appearing not to have heard – or choosing to ignore him – the woman called to a servant saying, "Whatever he tells you to do, do it."

Jesus sighed deeply. Then, pointing to six large stone pots, he said to servants nearby, "Fill the water pots with water."

Tobias and Rachel watched closely as servants went back and forth filling every pot to the brim. After all the pots were full, Jesus said, "Draw some out now and take it to the governor of the feast."

When the servants drew the first dipper, the children heard one of them say, "This water looks different." Another said, "It looks like wine."

A dip of a finger and a quick taste told the servants that the water was indeed now wine! They hurried to take it to the governor in charge of the wedding.

The children craned their necks to watch the governor of the feast taste the water turned into wine, and call out with delight to the bridegroom. They couldn't hear all that was said, but they saw the astonished expression on the bridegroom's face when he tasted the wine!

Soon servants were moving among the guests serving the new wine. The guests mingled with one another while sipping the wine saying, "Everyone brings forth the best wine first, then that which is worst. But this bridegroom saved the best for last."

Rachel said in a puzzled voice, "Tobias, I saw them pour water into the pots and now they're saying the water is wine. I don't understand."

"Neither do I!" Tobias said. "But somehow Jesus turned plain old water into good wine."

The children whispered about the mystery and enjoyed watching the festivities a while longer until a shadow began to darken the courtyard. Then Tobias said, "Come on, Rachel. We have to hurry to get back to the wagon."

They arrived just in time for Father to urge them into the wagon saying, "Good. You are back.

Did you enjoy yourselves?"

"Oh, yes, Father", the children chorused.

Their father smiled up at them." You may tell us all about what you did today while we eat tonight."

On the way home, Tobias and Rachel chattered about all they had seen – but most of all they talked about the water that was turned into wine. "Six water pots full, Rachel! The wedding feast was almost over and Jesus changed six pots of water into wine!" exclaimed Tobias.

"I wish we could have tasted some!" said Rachel. "Do you think it really was wine?"

"I'm sure it was. You heard the guests say it was even better than the wine served first."

They couldn't wait to share the amazing story.

But that night, while eating, as they told their parents and grandfather about the wedding and the miracle of the wine, their father broke in, "Nonsense! It was some kind of magic trick to entertain the guests. No one – not even God himself – can turn water into wine."

Softly Grandfather murmured, "I don't see why not. He turned water into blood when our people fled from Egypt didn't He?"

Chapter 3

A RUMOR

A few days later, Tobias practiced throwing clay dice while Rachel stood by her mother's loom begging to be allowed to throw the shuttle. "Please, Mama. I'll be careful. Just once?" she coaxed.

"Not this time, Rachel. This fabric is for a very important merchant. It has to be perfect."

Moments later, Grandfather returned from the market. He placed olive oil, a block of cheese, and dried fruits on the table. Breathing hard, he dropped heavily to rest on a stool.

The children scrambled to kneel before him. "Do you have a story for us, Grandfather?"

"Not a long story today, children, but I did hear some interesting things at the market."

"Tell us, Grandfather!" Rachel begged.

"Move closer to me, you three. I want to hear, too," Miriam chided.

Grandfather shifted his stool nearer to the loom; Tobias and Rachel scooted on their bottoms close to their mother's feet.

Once everyone was settled, Grandfather began, "It seems that man, Jesus, the one you saw at the wedding in Cana, is making quite a stir in Jerusalem," he said.

"He's turning more water into wine?" Tobias asked hopefully.

"No," Grandfather chuckled, "not that, but he's doing other things. People are saying that everywhere he goes, miracles take place."

"He's doing more miracles!" Miriam exclaimed. "What kind of miracles?"

"Well, healings for one thing. Blind people get back their sight; the lame walk, and deaf people hear again. Or so they say."

"Oh, Father," murmured Miriam. "How can that be? I never heard of such a thing."

"Well, we know about miracles from the Torah. Remember the story I told you children about Elisha and a boy who came back to life? But this is different. The gossip is that he only has to touch the sick and they are healed. In fact, I heard a woman say that people crowd around him hoping to touch him believing they will be healed.

One woman who had been sick for eighteen years crawled on her hands and knees just to touch the hem of his garment. And she was healed." Grandfather shrugged his shoulders. "Sometimes, they say, he doesn't even touch them! All he does is say the words, 'Be healed.'"

Tobias interrupted. "You mean he just says the words, 'Be healed' and people get well?" Tobias glanced at his own twisted foot wishing he could hear Jesus say those words to him.

"Well, sometimes he says to them, 'Your faith has made you whole.' That's not all. A woman named Mary from the village of Magdala claims that Jesus spoke to seven unclean spirits tormenting her and they left her."

"I've heard of Mary of Magdala," Miriam marveled. "She suffers so."

"Not any more. According to her, she has been set free."

"Jesus has power over demons? You mean all he has to do is speak to them and the evil spirits leave?" asked Tobias, shaking his curly head in wonder.

"The people in Jerusalem must be really happy he's helping them," Rachel chimed in.

"Not all the people, little one. Some even want to get rid of him. One time, I heard, Jesus and his disciples went to Jerusalem just before Passover. He went into the Temple area and, according to men who were there at the time, he created an awful uproar."

"He caused trouble in the Temple, Father! Whatever did he do?" Miriam asked.

"From what I heard, when he went into the Temple courtyard he saw oxen, sheep, and doves – animals for sacrifices – being sold. You know what it's like: money changers sitting at tables; people milling about, buying and selling. It seems that while Jesus watched the buying and selling, and the exchange of money, his hands were busy braiding small cords into a scourge, a whip."

Miriam paused in her weaving. "He made a scourge?" she asked. "Whatever did he want a scourge for?"

"Jesus used the scourge to drive the animals out of the Temple! Then he overturned the tables and poured out the money-changers' money. Oh, such commotion! There were animals charging through the court, coins clattering, and tables and chairs crashing. He shouted to those who sold doves, 'Take these things out of here; don't make my father's house a house of merchandise.' "

"Jesus must have been really angry," said Tobias, his black eyes sparkling as he pictured the scene in his mind.

"I imagine people were furious, too. Especially the ones doing the buying and selling," said Miriam.

"The merchants and money changers certainly were angry. But afterward many people gathered around Jesus and he began to teach them from the Scriptures. He said, 'Is it not written, my house shall be called by all nations the house of prayer, but you have made it a den of thieves.'

The authorities wanted to drive him out of Jerusalem, but because so many people thronged around him to hear his words and some to receive healing, the authorities couldn't get near him."

"Why did they want to drive him out, Grandfather?" asked

Tobias. "It seems like he was doing good, trying to keep the Temple a holy place."

"Good, yes. But remember what he said about the Temple? He called it 'my father's house.' Plainly he didn't mean his *earthly* father's house, and he certainly wouldn't call Herod, who is building the temple, his father. So he could only have meant that God himself is his father. That would make the priests very angry. Then, too, I suspect the chief priests and Pharisees might be afraid the people will start to follow Jesus instead of obeying them.

In any event, the men I talked with said that Jesus continued to teach in the Temple for a few days and then left Jerusalem. It wasn't safe for him there. They said he turned toward Galilee."

Miriam resumed weaving. "Well, well – so he may be coming our way again soon. Maybe we'll see some of these miracles ourselves!"

Chapter 4

A MYSTERY

While Miriam was polishing the metal mezuzah, her friend, Salome, appeared at the courtyard gate. As she straightened the mezuzah in place on the square wooden doorpost, Miriam smiled warmly. "Welcome home, Salome. What news do you have from Sychar?"

"My relatives are all well. It was good to see everyone and hear the family news. But," she added mysteriously, "family news isn't what I came to tell you!"

"No? Well come in and talk with me while we sit in the shade. I can't wait to hear."

Tobias and Rachel played nearby as the women settled on a bench beneath a tamarisk's feathery branches. Salome's eyes danced as she began to speak. "Miriam, I heard about the wedding in Cana and how Jesus turned water into wine. And to think that your Tobias and Rachel saw the whole thing! I also heard about the uproar when Jesus threw the money changers out of the temple. Well, now, listen to this: Jesus really stirred things up in Samaria!"

"Samaria? Why in the world was he there? Jews try to avoid going through Samaria."

"Don't I know it? It's not easy for my relatives to live so close to Samaritans and avoid contact with them. When Jesus left Judea to come back to Galilee, he and his disciples passed through Samaria rather than take the longer route.

They arrived near Shechem, about the sixth hour. When they came to Jacob's Well, Jesus was tired and thirsty. He sent the disciples into the city to buy food while he sat on the wall of the well to rest."

This promised suggestion of a story in the making drew Tobias and Rachel like moths to the flame of an oil lamp. They crept closer to the women in order to listen.

Salome went on. "While he rested, a Samaritan woman came along to draw water. My cousin told me the woman often came at that time because other women were unlikely to be there. You see, the woman had a bad reputation and other women of the village avoided her."

Rachel whispered, "Tobias, what's a bad reputation?"

"Not now!" Tobias silenced her. "I'll tell you later."

"The Samaritan woman said that Jesus asked her to give him water. She was surprised that he, a Jew, would ask her, a Samaritan, for a drink – and she said so! Do you know what Jesus replied? He said, 'If you knew the gift of God and who asked you for a drink, you would have asked him and he would have given you living water.'"

"Jesus would give her living water!" Miriam exclaimed. "Whatever did he mean? There's no running water near Jacob's Well is there?"

"No streams or springs that I know of. Anyway," Salome said, "I don't know what he meant about living water and neither did the Samaritan woman. She said she asked him where he would get this 'living water' and if he thought he was greater than Jacob who built the well."

Miriam chuckled and said, "Hmm. Not only does she have a bad reputation, she has a quick tongue! What did Jesus say to that?"

Salome paused for a moment, considering, before she went on with the story. "Then he said something even stranger. He said that anyone who drinks water from Jacob's Well will get thirsty again, but that whoever drinks his living water will never thirst again and that it will be a well of water in him giving eternal life."

"He said he had living water that gives eternal life! What kind of rabboni is this man?"

"The Samaritan woman claims he's not just a teacher, he's also a prophet. She said he told her all kinds of things about herself that he couldn't have known unless he was a prophet. Then he said something oddest of all. He said 'The hour is coming and now is when men will no longer worship in mountains or temples, that true worshipers will worship the Father in spirit and in truth'."

Tobias blinked. *There it was again! At the wedding Jesus had said, "My hour is not yet come." Now he says "the hour is coming and now is."*

Salome stood up to leave. "The Samaritan woman says she told Jesus that she knows the Messiah – the anointed One – is coming. And that when He comes, she said, he will tell us all things.

And now, listen to this," Salome leaned closer and went on. "Jesus said, 'I that speak to you am He.'"

"What!" Miriam blurted out. "Jesus claimed to be the Messiah? Isn't that blasphemy?"

"Well, if he's truly a prophet, and if he is who he claims to be, then maybe it's not blasphemy. Who knows? Anyhow, I must go now," she said moving toward the courtyard gate. "By the way, did you hear that Jonas, the nobleman's son, is sick with fever?"

"No, I didn't hear. Tobias is a friend of Jonas. I'll send him with some broth for Jonas later."

After Salome shut the gate and Miriam went back inside, Tobias sat very still. *My hour has not yet come. The hour is coming and now is. Men will not worship on mountains like the Samaritans do or in temples like the Jews. Is Jesus claiming to be the long awaited Messiah?*

Rachel broke into his thoughts, "Come on, Tobias. Let's finish the game."

"Go away, Rachel. I'm thinking."

Rachel huffed in disgust. Ever since Tobias had his eleventh birthday he was no fun at all!

CHAPTER 5

A HEALING

Rachel persisted in pestering Tobias. "Tobias. Tobias! Listen to me. I'm asking you a question."

"What is it now, Rachel?"

"What is a Messiah?"

"We learned that in synagogue school, Rachel."

"Not all girls go to synagogue school! Come on, Tobias, you'll have to tell me."

Tobias, about to say that girls didn't need to know such things, glanced at her trusting up-turned face and gave in. "All right. Messiah means Christ; the anointed one. The prophets had different ideas about the Messiah, but they all agreed that the Messiah will be a deliverer."

"What will the Messiah deliver people from, Tobias?"

"From all kinds of things, I guess. From the Romans, for sure, and who knows what else. Now leave me alone. I'm going to go to Jonas' house and see if Mother's soup made him feel better."

Jonas was nowhere to be seen when Tobias limped to the courtyard gate of Jonas' house. But there was some kind of excitement going on inside the gate. Jonas' father appeared to be upset as he instructed a servant. "Saddle an ass. My son is at the point of death! I must go to Cana to find Jesus. I've heard he is a healer."

Near death? Not Jonas! Tobias thought. He watched as

A Healing

Jonas' father urged the ass through the gate toward the road that led from Capernaum to Cana where it was rumored that Jesus was staying.

Tobias and a few other boys played quietly in the street outside Jonas' house waiting for word about their friend. They couldn't imagine that Jonas was sick enough to die. But they knew it must be bad if Jonas' father went to find Jesus.

The morning dragged on while the boys waited. Early in the afternoon a servant came out of the house and called to them. "The fever has broken! I go now to tell my master that his son lives." He hurried toward Cana as a loud cheer went up from the boys.

The following afternoon Tobias went again to Jonas' house hoping to see his friend up and about. Instead he found Jonas' father, returned from Cana, talking excitedly to his neighbors.

"I found Jesus. I asked him to come and heal my son who was dying. Jesus said, 'Unless you see signs and wonders, you won't believe.' I didn't know what he meant, but I said, 'Sir, come down lest my son dies.'

Then Jesus said, 'Go your way, your son lives.' I wanted to believe him. So I turned to come back to Capernaum the next morning. My servants met me on the way crying, 'Your son lives! The fever has broken. Jonas is alive!'"

Tears welled up in the father's eyes as he spoke. "Oh, the joy I felt! I asked the servants when Jonas began to get well. They told me the fever left him yesterday at the seventh hour. The seventh hour! Can you believe it? That was exactly the time Jesus said to me, 'Your son lives.'"

The neighbors began to murmur among themselves. "It was the exact same time?" "Jesus wasn't even near the boy." "He only spoke the words, 'Your son lives.'" "This is a miracle!"

"Yes! Yes!" Jonas' father exclaimed. "It *is* a miracle. And now I DO believe!" he cried out. "I believe as does my whole house!"

The neighbors left the courtyard, marveling at the miracle as they went, leaving Tobias alone with his thoughts. *What does Jonas' father believe? I know he believes the miracle. He believes in Jesus' power to heal. I wonder if he believes Jesus is the Messiah?*

Chapter 6

A Big Question

Tobias walked slowly, kicking small stones with the toe of his left sandal. He would much rather be outside in the warm sunshine than inside the musty synagogue learning the Torah. Lucky Rachel! While girls *could* go to synagogue school if they or their families wanted them to go, boys had no choice.

Nearing the synagogue, he saw people gathered around the porch. Eager to see what was happening, Tobias' limping pace quickened a little. He heard women's voices calling and begging, "Master!" "Master, touch my child." "Hold *my* baby, Master."

Curious about the cause of the women's excitement, Tobias jumped as high as he was able to try to see over the heads of the people. Once he caught a glimpse of Jesus seated on the synagogue steps. Jesus! Jesus was here at the synagogue! Women with children pushed others aside and pressed through the throng to reach the synagogue porch.

The instant a large man stepped to one side, Tobias saw his chance and squeezed through the break in the crowd. Wriggling through, he was able to make his way forward until he was close enough to Jesus that he could almost reach out and touch him.

A deep voice rose above the clamor of the mothers' voices. "Keep the children away."

The men who walked with Jesus began moving among the women saying, "Stay back." "Don't bother the Master." "Children stay away."

Tobias saw a frown crease Jesus' face before he called out, "Let the children come to me. Don't forbid them to come for such is the Kingdom of God. Truly I tell you whoever does not receive the Kingdom of God as a little child, he shall not enter in."

Tobias watched as Jesus took the children, one by one, in his arms and gently laid his hands on their heads to bless them. As he was returning the last child to her mother, Jesus lifted his eyes to look directly at Tobias.

Suddenly everything around Tobias faded away. It seemed like Jesus was looking right into his heart. What's more, he felt like Jesus knew everything there was to know about him – the good things and the not so good. Like how much Rachel irritated him. He even knew how it felt not to be able to run and play with the other boys.

But more than anything, Tobias saw love in Jesus' eyes. His smile spread warmth like liquid sunshine over Tobias. It seemed to flow from his head down to his feet. Oh, how he wished he were young enough to sit on Jesus' knees and feel his arms around him; to feel his hands on his head and hear his words of blessing.

Tobias did not go to synagogue school that day. When the mothers and children settled down around the feet of Jesus as he continued to teach, Tobias sat with them listening to every word. When Jesus finished teaching and rose from the steps to go on his way, it seemed to Tobias that the light of the day went with him.

Early that afternoon, Grandfather noticed that Tobias was unusually quiet. "What are you thinking about, Tobias?" he asked.

"I'm thinking about Jesus, Grandfather. He is back in

Capernaum. I saw him this morning at the synagogue. I heard he's staying at Peter the fisherman's house in Bethsaida. And …"Tobias' face glowed, "you know what, Grandfather? Jesus looked at me as if he knew me. Like he knew *me* – I mean *really* knew me. It seemed like he knew everything about me. And" Tobias said softly "he looked like … well, like he *loved* me, *truly* loved me. *Me*. And he doesn't even know my name!"

Grandfather waited for Tobias to say more.

"The men who were with him tried to keep children away, but Jesus said, 'Allow them to come.' Then he said that whoever doesn't receive the Kingdom of God as a little child cannot enter in. What is the Kingdom of God, Grandfather? And how can someone enter into it?"

"Well," said Grandfather, "a kingdom is where a king reigns; where he's the ruler. So the kingdom of God is where God reigns, where he is the ruler. Sometimes it's called the Kingdom of Heaven. The prophets tell us in the Torah that the time is coming when God will take up his perfect rule over the whole world and, even more, He will rule over men's hearts."

"Grandfather, I wish I knew more about the Kingdom and how to enter into it," said Tobias.

"Tobias, I don't know exactly what Jesus meant about receiving and entering into God's Kingdom, but I do have an idea of how we might find out. Let's go over to Bethsaida, let us see if we can find Jesus and maybe find out what he meant."

"Could we, Grandfather?" Tobias asked excitedly. "Could we go right now?"

"I don't see why not."

Within minutes a slim crippled boy and an old man were on their way to find answers to a big question.

Chapter 7

AN OFFERING

The streets of Bethsaida, a town on the north shore of the Sea of Galilee, were deserted. Jesus was nowhere to be found. Tobias and his grandfather wandered toward the fishing boats until they came upon a lone fisherman mending his nets. He told them that nearly everyone had followed Jesus to a hillside desert outside the city. He pointed the way while muttering to himself, "It seems like people would have something better to do than sit on a mountain and listen to stories!"

Tobias saw men, women and children dotting the mountainside overlooking the sea below. Jesus sat on a rock a little above the crowd. All eyes were turned toward him. All ears listened eagerly to his voice echoing in the stillness. Tobias and his grandfather picked their way through the crowd to find a spot as close as possible to Jesus and his disciples.

Jesus' teachings were like none Tobias had ever heard. "He's speaking in parables," Grandfather explained. Using stories about things the people were familiar with, the parables held their attention and the people seemed to understand them.

Most of the parables were about the Kingdom of Heaven, the very thing Tobias had asked Grandfather about. Tobias nudged his grandfather and they exchanged smiles. Maybe now they would learn more about the Kingdom of Heaven and how to enter into it!

Jesus told a story about a man who went out to sow seeds. He said some of the seed fell on stony ground, some fell among thorns. Only the seed that fell on good soil took root and produced fruit. Jesus explained that the seed is the word of the Kingdom, and the good ground is the one who hears the word and understands it. Listening to Jesus' words, Tobias hoped he was good soil.

All afternoon Jesus taught in parables about the Kingdom. He said the Kingdom of Heaven is like a mustard seed, the tiniest of seeds. Tobias thought about the mustard that grew on the garden plains of Gennesaret northwest of the Sea of Galilee. Often a mustard plant grew taller than any of the other herbs. Birds would perch on it to eat its' seed. Tobias wondered if Jesus meant that the Kingdom of Heaven would someday be the greatest kingdom of all.

When Jesus told the parable of the Kingdom of Heaven being like a woman who hid leaven in meal, Tobias thought about his mother putting a piece of dough from an earlier baking into meal when she was baking bread. Under the cover of a clean cloth, the piece of dough was hidden. Tobias couldn't see it working, but at the right time, when the cloth was removed, the bowl overflowed with dough ready to be formed into loaves and put in the oven. Maybe, Tobias hoped, that meant that the Kingdom of Heaven, though now hidden like the leaven, would grow in his understanding.

Tobias loved the parable of the pearl of great price. Jesus said the pearl was so precious a man was willing to sell everything he had to get it. He said that's how precious the Kingdom of Heaven is.

The sun was low in the sky when Jesus finished teaching. Tobias heard the disciples say to him, "Master, send the people away so they can go to the villages and get something to eat."

Jesus answered, "They don't need to leave. You feed them."

"But, Master," the disciples protested. "We have no food to feed all these people."

Jesus asked, "What do you have?"

A young boy not far from Tobias said softly to a disciple standing near, "Sir, I have five barley loaves and two fishes."

The disciple laughed and said, "Master, here's a lad willing to give his five loaves and two fishes."

"Bring them to me," Jesus said. He took the loaves and fishes, held them up, and looking toward heaven, he blessed them. Then he broke them and said, "Take and feed the people."

Take only five barley loaves and two small fishes to feed a multitude of thousands? What was Jesus thinking? But the disciples obeyed.

They moved among the people, giving each as much as they wanted, and the food never ran out. When all had been fed, Jesus told the disciples to gather up the fragments so that none would be lost. The leftover fragments of barley loaves filled twelve baskets!

Tobias could hardly believe his eyes. Jesus multiplied five barley loaves and two fishes to work a miracle to feed thousands of people. He and Grandfather had eaten miracle food; Kingdom food!

When Jesus realized that the people wanted to make him a king, he told his disciples to go down the mountain and get in a ship to go to Capernaum while he went up the mountain to be alone. Jesus sent the multitude away and slowly the people began to make their way off the mountain to return to their homes.

Tobias was very quiet as they walked home from Bethsaida. Grandfather was careful not to interrupt his thoughts. Finally Tobias said, "Grandfather, is this part of what entering the Kingdom of Heaven is about? Giving all we have? The boy gave what he had and Jesus blessed it and it was more than enough to feed everyone."

"Perhaps that is part of it, Tobias."

"But, Grandfather, only God himself could do a miracle like that."

"Well, some are saying that Jesus is the Messiah, the Son

of God. And" Grandfather smiled, "the Book of Psalms tells us that God will speak to us in parables. Perhaps we just heard His voice."

Chapter 8

A MIRACLE

Early the next morning, Miriam gave Tobias coins to buy fish fresh from the night's catch at the fish market. The black volcanic rock hills rising behind the stony beach reflected the morning light. Pelicans soared and folded their wings to swoop and scoop fish into their massive bills. More boats than Tobias had ever seen at one time lined the shore.

Then Tobias saw Jesus. He was standing apart from the crowd talking with his disciples. Fishermen clustered in small groups amid the boats talking loudly to one another.

Curious, Tobias moved among the fishermen catching snatches of conversations. The men's voices sounded puzzled. "How can it be?" one asked. "I myself saw the disciples go *down* the mountain to the only boat on shore and I watched Jesus go further *up* the mountain.

Another responded, "If the disciples took the only boat to row across to this side, how did Jesus get here?"

"The disciples left the mountain at dusk," said still another. "Before dawn this morning, boats came in from all directions bringing people who heard that Jesus was teaching on the mountain. When they saw that Jesus wasn't there anymore, they thought he had gone with the disciples. So they began rowing to meet him over here on this side of the lake. And here they are," he said sweeping his arm toward them. "And there's Jesus"

A Miracle

"The disciples must have rowed back to get him," said one of the younger men.

"No," a rough voice from the edge of the group said. "The disciples insist they didn't go back for Jesus. He came to them."

"Came to them? How could he do that without a boat?" asked a bearded burly man dragging his net behind him.

Tobias listened carefully. He heard the rough voice continue, "The disciples say they were half-way across the lake when a strong gale blew in and the sea became rough. Their boat was being tossed every which way. That's when they saw something moving on the water toward them. At first they were frightened and cried out, 'It's a spirit!'

But right away, they said, a voice spoke to them saying, 'Fear not. It is I.' Jesus was walking on the water toward them!"

A man in the crowd shouted, "This isn't the Dead Sea, you know! No man can walk on water, not even on water as salty as that!"

In the hush that followed, the man telling the story went on. "Well, I don't know. Another man *nearly* walked on water. The disciples saw that when they heard Jesus' voice, Peter called out, 'If it is you, Master, let me come to you on the water.' They said that Jesus held out his hand to Peter saying, 'Come.'"

"What did Peter do?" asked a woman standing near the speaker.

"Peter stepped out of the boat and began walking on the water to go to Jesus! But," and now he chuckled, "when Peter saw that the wind was stronger and the sea rougher, he was afraid. Beginning to sink, he cried out, 'Lord, save me!'"

The men laughed heartily saying, "That sounds like Peter! So what happened?"

"Jesus stretched out his hand, caught Peter, and said to him, 'O you, of little faith, why did you doubt?' When he and Peter were both back in the boat, the wind stopped blowing!"

Now the storyteller paused for effect. When he was sure he had everyone's attention, he said, "Then the disciples worshipped Jesus saying, 'Truly, you are the Son of God.'"

As the story of Peter walking on water and the disciples' confession spread throughout the crowd gathered on the shore, excitement and a sense of awe grew among them. They all wanted to draw closer to Jesus, to reach out and touch Him, some hoping to be healed.

Tobias was so excited about the miracle of Jesus walking on water … he forgot all about the fish he had been sent to buy.

CHAPTER 9

A LESSON

Rachel ran to meet Tobias when he returned later that morning. "You're in big trouble, Tobias," she piped. "You better repent for what you *didn't* do!"

"Oh, be quiet Rachel!" Tobias retorted, only then remembering the forgotten fish. At the sound of his mother's sandals shuffling on the clay floor, he turned to see her frown and to hear her demand, "Tobias! Where have you been? And where are the fish I sent you to buy?"

Shamefaced, Tobias said, "I'm sorry, Mother. I forgot all about the fish."

Forgot? Miriam thought. *Tobias, my responsible son, forgot?*

Grandfather looked up from where he sat mending leather sandals. "What happened that was important enough to make you forget, Tobias?"

Tobias began to tell them about all that he had heard and seen. His father came in as he was telling about Peter's attempt to walk on water.

"Did *you* see Jesus and Peter walking on water?" Father asked.

"No. But I saw Peter still wet from the dunking. And the way the other disciples teased him and all told the same story, I believe it's true."

"I see." Father said. "Go on. What did you do then?" he

asked as he lowered himself to sit on a wooden bench.

"I listened to the men talk some more about Jesus walking on the water and I watched as people seemed to come from everywhere to see Jesus and to ask for healing."

"Did Jesus heal them?" Father asked.

"He healed many of them. Some got well just by reaching out and touching his robe," Tobias said. Tobias looked thoughtful as he went on to say, "But Jesus seemed bothered, too."

"Bothered?" Grandfather asked. "Bothered about what?"

"Well, for one thing. He told the people that they didn't look for him because of the miracles, but because they ate the bread and were filled. He said they shouldn't look for bread that won't last, but for the bread of everlasting life."

"Did anyone ask him how to find that bread?" asked Miriam.

"No," said Tobias, laughing, "but one man said that our fathers ate manna in the desert; bread from heaven. Then Jesus said, 'Truly I tell you that Moses didn't give your fathers that bread from heaven; my Father gives you the true bread from heaven.'"

"True bread?" asked Rachel. "What other kind of bread is there?"

"Jesus said that the true bread is He who came down from heaven and gives life to the whole world."

Father said, "Go on, Tobias. What else did Jesus say?"

"He said, 'I am the Bread of Life. Whoever comes to me will never be hungry, and whoever believes on me will never thirst.'"

"That's almost like what he told the Samarian woman!" Miriam exclaimed.

"I AM", Grandfather murmured. "Jesus said, '*I am* the bread of life.' The same word Yahweh told Moses to use to tell the Egyptians that I AM sent him."

Chapter 10

A THREAT

Tobias sat in a quiet spot under an olive tree a little way from the house. He folded his arms on his drawn up knees, and rested his chin on his arms. At last he was able to be alone to think about all that had happened over the past months. There was a lot to think about!

He thought about hearing the men on shore say that when the disciples realized it was Jesus walking toward them on the water, they said to him, "Truly you are the Son of God."

Tobias also thought about a time when Jesus taught on a hillside that his disciples, noticing that Jesus often went off by himself to pray, said to him, "Master, teach us to pray." And Jesus said, "When you pray, say our Father who art in heaven."

This was the first time Tobias – or anyone else for that matter – had heard God referred to as Father. And the word Jesus used was not the usual one. He used the word Abba; the same loving word Tobias and Rachel sometimes used for their father. "Daddy."

Tobias knew that God's name was so holy it couldn't ever be spoken or even written. Only the letters YWH were ever written and from them came the spoken word Yahweh. But Jesus said to pray, "Our Daddy God, who art in heaven."

Tobias felt that made God seem not so far off, but up close and real. Like you could climb right up, sit on his knee, and whisper in his ear! The same way that, so many months ago, Tobias had longed to sit on Jesus' lap and feel his arms around him.

The disciples said they were to pray that God's Kingdom would come and that His will would be done on earth just like it was in heaven. *When would that be?* Tobias wondered. *How would God's Kingdom come? What would it be like?*

It seemed like Jesus was always talking about the Kingdom of God. He said the Kingdom of Heaven was *near*, that you could *enter* the kingdom of God, and that the kingdom of God was *in you*.

Such heavy thoughts made Tobias' twelve year old head hurt!

People from both near and far followed Jesus everywhere. Sometimes, to get away from the press of people, Jesus taught from a boat a short way from the shore. Other times he went into the mountains alone to pray. But, even then, people followed him and Jesus never turned anyone away. He treated everyone the same: old, young, rich, or poor.

Tobias was often one of those following after Jesus. He wanted to be near him; to listen to his teachings. Besides, something exciting always seemed to happen when Jesus was around!

One time Grandfather was with Tobias when they saw a crowd of people gathered outside a house where Jesus was staying. There were so many people trying to get inside, the doorway was blocked. No one could get in or out of the house.

"Look, Grandfather," Tobias said, pointing to four men who were carrying a crippled man on a pallet toward the house. "They'll never be able to get in."

But to Tobias' surprise, the men carried the pallet up the outer staircase to the rooftop. After setting the pallet on the roof, they began removing tiles to create an opening in the roof large enough to allow them to let the pallet down to the room below.

"I wish we could see inside, Grandfather."

"As do I, Tobias. But I think we both have a pretty good idea what's going on in there."

Sometime later, after the crowd had thinned, they were still there when the once crippled man walked through the open door carrying his pallet. Amid the chorus of "ooh's" and "aah's", Tobias barely heard his grandfather's awed voice, "Look! He's healed, Tobias! The crippled man is walking."

Oh, Jesus, Tobias thought, "*If only you could heal my crooked foot!*

Chapter 11

A RULE BREAKER

As time went by, Tobias began to see that Jesus was different from most rabboni in ways other than healing the sick. For one thing, he didn't always follow the rules: the Pharisees' rules!

One Sabbath morning, Tobias left his family after worship at the neighborhood synagogue to take a longer path home. As he passed by a cornfield, he saw Jesus and some of his disciples in the field. The hungry disciples were plucking ears of corn from the stalks, rubbing the ears in their hands to eat the ripe kernels.

Pharisees, walking the same path, also saw the disciples, and approached Jesus saying, "Your disciples do what it is not lawful to do on the Sabbath day." Tobias shivered at the sound of harsh voices and flinched at the scowls on angry faces.

But Jesus answered in a calm voice. "Have you not read what David did when he and those with him were hungry? How he entered the house of God and ate the shewbread in the Holy Place of the tabernacle; bread that was meant only for the priests? I tell you that here in this place is one greater than the temple. If you had known what God meant when he said I will have mercy, not sacrifice, you wouldn't condemn the guiltless. For the Son of Man is Lord even of the Sabbath day."

Tobias' heart skipped a beat. *Was Jesus saying that he was greater than the temple? Was he saying that he was Lord of the Sabbath day? What would the authorities do to him if these Pharisees told them what Jesus said?*

That same evening Tobias' family returned to the synagogue for worship. As they took their places a commotion at the door caught their attention. Jesus was entering the synagogue. So were some Pharisees. The Pharisees watched with narrowed eyes as a man with a withered hand began to walk toward Jesus.

Tobias held his breath. He knew the Pharisees were watching to see whether Jesus would heal the man on the Sabbath. Jesus looked lovingly at the man with the withered hand and said, "Stand forth."

Then he turned to the Pharisees and asked, "Is it lawful to do good on the Sabbath day, or to do evil; to save life, or to kill?" The Pharisees didn't answer; their faces were stony cold. Tobias saw a flicker of anger cross Jesus' face at their hardness of heart.

Then Jesus said to the man, "Stretch forth your hand." He stretched it out and immediately his hand was made whole. Now the cold faces of the Pharisees burned with hatred.

When Tobias' father heard one of the Pharisees say to the others, "Come. We will take counsel with the Herodians, how we might destroy him," he muttered to Miriam, "Now what are they up to? The Herodians are wealthy Jews who support Herod. They don't want to hear anything about the coming Messiah. But Jesus has done no wrong."

Tobias' heart was heavy. He was afraid for Jesus, terribly afraid. He thought about Jesus' words, "Blessed are you when you are persecuted for righteousness sake." Tobias trembled. He was fearful that the persecution Jesus spoke of was beginning.

On the way home after the service, Miriam spoke up,

"Jesus seems like a good man and he isn't hurting anyone – he's helping people. Why are the authorities so against him?"

Grandfather put his arm around Miriam and said, "Daughter, jealousy and fear make men do strange things. Besides, they think illness is caused by sin, so, they reason, how can Jesus – who they think is himself a sinner – heal others?"

"Is sickness caused by sin?" Rachel asked with a worried expression, thinking about the scratchiness she was beginning to feel in her throat.

Grandfather laughed, "No, but your question reminds me of something, Rachel. Tobias, remember the day – not so long ago – when we were there when a man who had been blind since the day he was born, passed by Jesus?"

"I remember, Grandfather. The disciples asked Jesus who sinned, the man or his parents that he was born blind."

"And Jesus answered, 'Neither the man or his parents sinned, but that the works of God should be seen in him.' Tell Rachel what Jesus did next, Tobias."

"He spit on the ground and made clay. Then he spread the clay on the eyes of the blind man."

"Ugh," said Rachel.

"The blind man didn't think it was ugly," said Grandfather. "Jesus told him to go and wash in the pool of Siloam. He did. And when he came back, he could see."

"And you witnessed this?" asked Father.

"Yes. Oddly enough, this healing also happened on the Sabbath. When his neighbors asked how his eyes were opened, the once blind man told them what had happened.

I heard later that they took the man before the Pharisees. When the scribes and Pharisees asked him how he had received his sight, he said 'A man put clay upon my eyes and I washed and now do see.' They asked him what he had to say about Jesus, and he said 'He is a prophet.'

But the Jews didn't believe his story, so they called forth his parents and asked them if the man was their son and how it was that he could now see."

"They must have believed his parents," said Miriam.

"Well, sorry to say, the parents were afraid of the Jews; they were afraid they would be put out of the synagogue if they said that Jesus healed their son, so they said they didn't know! They said their son was of age, so ask him."

"They lied!" gasped Rachel.

"Yes, they lied," said Grandfather. "So then the Pharisees said to the man, 'Give God the praise. We know this man, Jesus, is a sinner.' "

"As we all are," said Father. "What happened then?"

"Well, the man healed of blindness said, 'I do not know whether he is a sinner or not. One thing I know; I was blind, now I see.' "

Tobias' father dropped his head and in a very low voice said, "O God, have I, too, been blind and am only now beginning to see?"

Chapter 12

A Raising

Jesus gave his disciples power to cast out demons and heal the sick in his Name. He himself taught and ministered throughout Galilee. He appointed seventy of his followers to go before him to prepare village people for his arrival.

As Jesus' fame spread by word of mouth, he was seen less often in Capernaum. Tobias missed seeing him and hearing his voice. But mostly he missed the warm feeling he had when Jesus was near.

Men, including Tobias' father and grandfather, began to meet in one another's homes or under the shade of trees, away from the eyes of the authorities, to discuss Jesus' teachings. Sometimes one or more of the disciples met with them. Tobias wished he were old enough to join the men. Whenever he could, he drew near enough to listen to them.

Tobias loved it when a disciple's answer to a question began with the words, "The Master says ..." Some of those times he felt like the teachings were meant especially for him.

Like the time when Peter said, "I asked the Master how many times we should forgive someone who sins against us. I thought He would say seven times. But He said, 'I say not unto thee seven times, but until seventy times seven.'"

Right away Tobias thought of the mean boys who taunted him about his lameness, saying things like, "Who sinned

Tobias, you or your parents?" Or times when they called Tobias names like Gimpy or Limp-Along.

Grandfather said he should just ignore them. But it was hard to ignore them – when he wanted to punch them in the nose! The name calling hurt and Tobias hated them for it.

But Jesus says he should *forgive* them; not just once but many times?

"Jesus says we should love our enemies and pray for them and if one strikes you, you should turn the other cheek," said Peter. Tobias squirmed uncomfortably and not from the prickly bushes he was sitting under. It was hard enough to ignore his tormenters. He wasn't at all sure he could *forgive* them, let alone love them and pray for them.

Another time Tobias listened as his grandfather asked John what Jesus would say was the greatest commandment in the law. John said that a lawyer asked Jesus that same question, hoping to trap him. Jesus said, "Thou shalt love the Lord thy God with all thy heart, with all thy soul, with all thy mind and with all thy strength. This is the first and great commandment and the second is like it. Thou shalt love thy neighbor as thyself."

The boys who tormented him were his neighbors. How, Tobias wondered, *could he love them?*

One evening some followers met at the home of Tobias and his family. The disciple, Thomas, was with them. Tobias longed to join them on the rooftop. Rachel gave him a shove saying, "Oh Tobias, why don't you just go up there and listen?"

"No, silly, I can't. I'm not old enough yet to sit with the men and I'm certainly not going to sit with the women! I'm going to crouch here on the steps and listen. And you keep quiet!"

Tobias moved a few steps higher to hear a man say to Thomas, "We heard something about a man from Bethany named Lazarus who Jesus raised from the dead. Of course, it can't be true. Can it?"

"It is true," said Thomas. Thomas told that after Jesus had narrowly escaped being taken, he got word that his dear friend, Lazarus, was sick. Jesus loved Lazarus and his two sisters, Mary and Martha, but waited two days before he said, 'Let us go to them.' "

"Why did Jesus wait?" asked Father.

Thomas said he and the other disciples tried to convince Jesus not to go to Judea at all because it was there the Jews had tried to stone him. But Jesus said that Lazarus was sleeping and that he would awake him from sleep. The disciples said if he was sleeping, he would do well. Then Jesus said plainly, "Lazarus is dead."

When the disciples realized that Jesus was determined to go, even though it was too late to help Lazarus, Thomas said, "Let us go also that we may die with him."

"Did you really think that you might be stoned, Thomas?"

"Yes! His enemies are determined to do away with the Master. If they stoned Him to death they would stone us, too."

Bethany, said Thomas, was about two miles from Jerusalem. When they arrived, Lazarus had been in the grave four days.

Many Jews had gathered to comfort Mary and Martha. Thomas said that when they saw Jesus some of the Jews said, "Couldn't this man who opened the eyes of the blind have kept this one whom he loved from dying?" Even the two sisters told Jesus that if he had been there, their brother would not have died.

One of the women listening to Thomas said, "That must have made Jesus feel terrible."

"He did feel terrible," said Thomas. "When they took him to the grave site, he wept. Then he said to Martha, 'Take the stone away.' But Martha said, 'Lord, by this time he stinks for he's been dead four days.'"

"I would think he would!" agreed the men. "So what did they do?"

"They rolled the stone away! Jesus told Martha if she would only believe she would see the glory of God. Then, in a loud voice, he said, 'Lazarus, come forth!'"

"And?" clamored several of the men.

Now Thomas practically shouted. "Then ... Lazarus came forth, bound hand and foot with grave clothes, even his face was covered with a napkin. And Jesus said, 'Loose him and let him go.'"

There were a few moments of awed silence; then shouts went up. "Glory to God!" "Praise be to Yahweh!" "Hallelujah!"

When the shouts died down, a man wearing a worried expression, asked, "What did the Jews do when they saw that Lazarus was alive?"

Tobias strained to hear the answer to this final question.

"Many of the Jews who saw what Jesus had done believed on Him," Thomas said. "But others of them went on their ways to the Pharisees, to tell them what they had seen," Thomas replied in a somber voice.

Chapter 13

A QUESTION

Weeks and months passed. Tobias grew more and more fearful for Jesus. Every few days, it seemed, there was a new report of an attempt by the scribes and Pharisees to trap him into saying or doing something they could use against him. Even worse were the reports of actual attempts on his life. From the time they heard of Lazarus being raised from the dead, the chief priests and Pharisees plotted to kill Jesus.

One day, when Tobias was helping his Father prepare fabrics for market, he asked, "What are the authorities trying to do to Jesus, Father? Why do they keep asking him trick questions?"

"They're hoping to get him to say something that they can use to accuse him of blasphemy."

"But isn't blasphemy saying bad or untrue things about God? Jesus would never do that! He says God is his heavenly father – his Abba."

"True. I don't believe he would either. But once when they questioned him about God he said, 'Before Abraham was, I am.' He used the same word that God spoke to Moses long ago, saying 'Tell the people that I AM has sent me unto you.' And the very words he used when he said 'I AM the bread of life'. Scribes and Pharisees thought he was saying that he was God. They took up stones to cast at him then."

Now Father smiled broadly, "But Jesus hid himself from them and went out of the temple, walking right through the midst of them. They didn't even see him!"

"He walked right by them and they didn't even see him!" Tobias said with a grin.

Just then Rachel entered the shed. "Can I help?" she asked. Father looked at her grubby hands. "Not today, Rachel."

"But Tobias is helping!"

"Tobias will soon be thirteen – a man. He'll be old enough to help me with the business."

Turning to Tobias again, Father said, "You see, that's another thing that angers the authorities. Jesus often says that he must be about his father's business. Once he said to them, 'You say I blaspheme because I said I am the Son of God? If I don't do the works of my Father, don't believe me. But if I do, even though you don't believe me, believe the works that I do, so that you may know that the Father is in me, and I am in Him.' Once again they tried to take him, but he escaped out of their hand."

And Tobias remembered Jesus saying, "My time is not yet come."

Later, while eating the evening meal, Rachel asked, "Father, do you believe that Jesus is the Son of God?"

Miriam laid her hand on Rachel's head and said, "You may be a small girl, but you do know how to ask big questions!"

Father laid aside his napkin and said firmly, "A couple of years ago I would have scoffed at your question, Rachel. But now, seeing what we've seen and hearing all that we've heard about Jesus, I must say, 'Yes' I do believe Jesus is the Son of God. Nothing else makes sense."

"And think about what the disciples told us about being with Jesus, Moses, and Elijah on the mountain top." said Grandfather. "They said they saw Jesus in a radiant white robe standing with Moses and Elijah. It seems like the law and the prophets were coming together with Jesus."

"If that's so, then Jesus *is* the long-awaited Messiah," said Tobias.

"Many say so," said Father. Then, taking a deep breath, he went on, "And I am one of them. Messiah means Christ, the anointed one. Jesus couldn't do all that he does without being anointed and empowered by God."

"We're taught that the Messiah will be King of the Jews. That he'll be a leader who will defeat our enemies and bring a time of peace and prosperity," said Grandfather.

"But Grandfather," Rachel asked in a small voice. "Who are our enemies?"

"Well, the Romans for one," he answered. "They have us under their thumb. And, now, if we believe Jesus is the Messiah, then the scribes and Pharisees are our enemies as well as His."

A chill brought goose bumps as Tobias considered the danger that Jesus and his followers, followers that included himself and his family, now faced.

Chapter 14

A Touch

Several days later, Tobias spotted what looked like a heap of cloth crumpled alongside the path on his return from synagogue school. As he neared the heap, he was surprised to see the cloth move. Then he heard a whimpering sound. As he came even nearer, he realized that it was not a pile of cloth, but a person; a person rocking back and forth and moaning. It was Jason, the leader of the pack of boys who taunted Tobias at every opportunity. He was holding his ankle with both hands.

Tobias was tempted to pass him by, but when he saw that Jason was crying he knelt beside him and asked. "Are you hurt, Jason? What happened?"

Jason said, "We were playing tag. I stepped on a rock and turned my ankle. It hurts something awful."

"Let me see," said Tobias. Jason's ankle was swollen and hot to the touch.

"Where are the other boys?" asked Tobias.

"They ran off when they saw me fall. I can't put my weight on my foot; it hurts too much. Maybe it's broken," he whimpered.

"I can't tell if it's broken," said Tobias, "but we need to get you home."

"I can't walk on it," protested Jason.

"I know, but if you can get up on your other leg and put

The Hour Is Now

your arm around my shoulder, you can hop on one foot."

"But you ..."

"I know. I have a bad leg, too. But between us we have two good legs! We can do it."

Tobias helped Jason stand up and balance on one leg. He put his arm around Jason's waist and Jason laid his arm around Tobias' shoulder. In spite of a few false starts and stumbles, they were able to walk together with Tobias bearing most of Jason's weight and Jason hopping on one foot.

As they made their way toward Jason's home, Jason asked, "Why did you stop to help me, Tobias? You didn't have to. We haven't exactly been friends."

Tobias remembered the parable Jesus told about the Samaritan who helped a Jew when priests and Pharisees passed him by. "I think it's what Jesus would want me to do," he said.

"Jesus? What does Jesus have to do with us?" Jason asked.

"Jesus is God's own Son. He teaches His followers how God wants us to live so that we can be part of His kingdom."

"Are you a follower of Jesus?"

Tobias thought for only a moment before answering. "Yes, I am. At least, I know I want to be."

Jason said nothing for a few minutes. When they neared his home, he mumbled, "Tobias, thank you for helping me. I - I'm sorry I've been so mean to you."

Tobias said softly, "Jason, I forgive you." Jason dropped his head and nodded as he hobbled inside.

As Tobias spoke the words, "I forgive you", he thought he felt someone's hand on his shoulder. But when he turned to see who touched him, he saw no one. Strangely, even though it was a cool day, he suddenly felt warm all over.

Puzzled, Tobias turned to walk away. But when he stepped out on his lame foot, he realized he was no longer limping. His foot and ankle were perfectly straight!

He took another step. And then another. He was walking!

Tobias realized that the hand he thought he had felt was not his imagination. It was real. It was the hand of Jesus! As

Jesus had healed so many others, He had healed him.

He, Tobias, had been touched by the Son of God.

And he would never be the same.

Filled with joy Tobias walked faster – and then faster. Soon he was running, and leaping, and laughing out loud as he raced toward home.

Bursting into the house, Tobias shouted, "Grandfather, Father, Mother, Rachel – everyone! – look at me!"

The family rushed to see what all the shouting was about. To their amazement, Tobias began prancing around the house, hopping on one foot and then the other, spinning in circles.

Rachel screamed, "Tobias, you're not limping!"

Miriam said, "Glory be to God!" and began crying while Father demanded to know what had happened.

Tobias told them about Jason, his hurt foot and ankle, and how he helped him get home. When he got to the part about Jason asking why he had stopped to help him and then, later, saying he was sorry for being so mean to Tobias, Father's eyes glistened.

Tobias' voice softened when he repeated the words he spoke to Jason, saying "I forgive you." His voice grew husky when he told his family about feeling a hand on his shoulder and feeling warm all over.

"Who was it, Tobias? Who touched you?" Rachel demanded.

"When I turned around to see, Rachel, there was no one there."

Miriam whispered, "It was Jesus."

Tobias nodded. "Yes, Mother. It was Jesus. That's when I realized that my foot and ankle were straight and that Jesus had healed me."

No one spoke for a few minutes; awed by what Jesus had done. Then Grandfather looked into Tobias' eyes and said, "Tobias, I believe Jesus healed more than just your foot today."

Chapter 15

A JOURNEY

The days and weeks sped by as Tobias approached his thirteenth birthday. Days filled with the joy of being able to run, play games, and join the other boys in activities he had so longed to be part of. When asked why he no longer limped, he simply said, with a wide smile, "Jesus healed me!"

One spring day, Grandfather was busy making still another pair of sandals for Tobias. As he stitched the leather thongs to the sole, he said, "Tobias, you wear these out faster than I can make them!"

"I know, Grandfather," Tobias replied. "My tunic is short, too! Isn't it wonderful?"

"It is indeed, Grandson. Just think, tomorrow you will be of age."

Hearing their voices, Father entered the room. "That's true. I've been thinking that this year we three should go to Jerusalem to observe Passover."

"Father, do you mean it? That I'm to go, too?" Tobias asked.

"The Torah requires that every man observe Passover at least once at the Temple. You will be of age, thirteen, Tobias, and what better time than now for three generations to observe Passover together in Jerusalem? I also must deliver an order of linen there to Joseph of Arimathea."

Tobias asked excitedly, "When will we leave, Father?"

"We will leave early the day before the Sabbath to arrive in

A Journey

Bethany late in the afternoon. We'll stay with your uncle Abe and his family. With his boys and his daughters' husbands there will be nine men and you, Tobias, will make the required tenth to celebrate Passover." His father's words made Tobias feel at least two inches taller!

"Rather than take the route along the Jordan River, we'll travel the Roman road. It's a more direct route and the paved road will make it easier for the mules to pull the cart. Besides, we should get some use from the high taxes we pay. Also, for safety, we can join a caravan of others traveling to Jerusalem.

Now, men, we have only a few short days to get ready, so come on, let's get busy!"

The sun was barely above the horizon when the cart loaded with fabric for delivery and provisions for the day's journey pulled away from the house. Miriam and Rachel waved from the rooftop, although Rachel was not happy about being left behind.

The road was crowded with travelers; some walking, others riding on mules or, rarely, on horses, and many were riding on carts or in wagons. It was about 70 miles as the crow flies from Capernaum to Jerusalem. Bouncing along in the cart, Tobias thought about Jesus. He and the disciples traveled on foot and Tobias knew Jesus avoided the Roman roads, taking the foot paths along the Jordan instead.

It must have taken Jesus days to walk from Capernaum to Jerusalem. Tobias tried to imagine walking, walking, walking the dusty roads with only what he could carry for provisions or with no provisions at all. Tobias wondered where Jesus slept. He heard Jesus say once that the Son of Man had no place to lay his head.

The last rays of light fell as they turned from the main road to take a side route to the little town of Bethany. They would need to move a little faster if they were to reach Uncle Abe's before the Sabbath began at sundown.

As they approached the town, Tobias saw flat roofed stone homes scattered around the shoulder of a small mountain. "That's the Mount of Olives," said Grandfather. "Abe's house is just ahead."

Chapter 16

A CELEBRATION

The next day, the Sabbath, was quiet. After the long day of traveling, it was nice to spend time resting and getting to know his cousins whom he didn't see very often. It was fun to be the center of attention when he told his relatives about his healing. And even more so when they clapped him on the shoulder and exclaimed over his ability to walk and run. He thought Uncle Abe would never stop asking him questions about it!

The morning after the Sabbath, Tobias explored the small town of Bethany tucked in the shoulder of the Mount. As he wandered the streets, he noticed people gathering on the footpath leading down the mountain toward Jerusalem. Curious, he ran to see what was happening.

As he neared the small crowd he saw a man riding on a donkey. Men walked alongside him. When he drew closer, Tobias was overjoyed to see that the man riding the donkey was Jesus and the men with him were his disciples.

Tobias tore back to his uncle's home. Grandfather, Father and Uncle Abe were sharing stories when Tobias broke into their conversation, shouting, "Jesus is here! I just saw him riding on a donkey toward Jerusalem; his disciples are with him."

"Strange," said Uncle Abe. "Jesus often stays with Mary, Martha, and Lazarus, his good friends, when he's in Bethany.

But usually not all his disciples are with him. And I've never once seen Jesus riding a donkey. He must have come for Passover in Jerusalem. But I wonder why he's riding in on a donkey?"

"Can we go with them?" begged Tobias. "Please."

"I don't see why not," said Uncle Abe. "It's only a Sabbath Day's journey from here to Jerusalem. Not far; only about 2000 cubits. Let's join them and see what's going on."

By the time they caught up with Jesus, a small crowd had gathered to walk with him. The disciples had put their cloaks on the donkey for Jesus to sit upon. People were cutting branches of palm trees from the lower levels of Mount Olive to wave as Jesus went by. Others waving palm branches, ran toward Jesus and his followers from the direction of Jerusalem. Still others were casting branches and garments of clothes on the path in front of the donkey.

"What are they doing?" asked Tobias.

"I have no idea," said Uncle Abe. "I've never seen anything like this before."

"Listen to the people shouting," said Grandfather.

Voices rang out. "Hosanna!"

"Blessed is the King of Israel that cometh in the name of the Lord!"

"Peace in heaven and glory in the highest!"

"Save us, Jesus!"

Grandfather grasped Father's arm and laid a hand on Tobias' shoulder, "The prophet Zechariah foretold this day five hundred years ago!"

What do you mean, Grandfather? How could he know about this day?"

"Remember what I told you about prophets, Tobias? They hear from God and speak what they hear. When Zachariah said, *'Rejoice greatly, O daughter of Zion: shout, O daughter of Jerusalem, behold thy King cometh unto thee: he is just, and having salvation: lowly, and riding upon an ass, and upon a colt the foal of an ass,'* he was speaking of this very day."

Father's voice caught as he said, "The fulfillment of this

prophecy is one more proof that Jesus *is* our long-awaited Messiah."

"And to think that we are here to see it together," said Uncle Abe.

"And to think that I have lived to see this day!" said Grandfather. "We are of all men, blessed of God."

Tobias snatched up a palm branch from the path and ran toward Jesus, waving the branch high in the air and shouting with the others, "Jesus!" "King Jesus!" "Hosanna!" "Blessed is He that comes in the name of the Lord." "Hosanna in the highest!"

But not everyone was singing praises.

Pharisees among the crowd, said to Jesus, "Master, rebuke your disciples." Tobias grinned when he heard Jesus answer them, saying, "I tell you that if these held their peace, the stones would cry out."

The joyous crowd, including Grandfather, Father and Uncle Abe followed along all the way to Jerusalem. Tobias ran ahead of them, waving his palm branch and shouting "Messiah! The Messiah has come!"

But when they arrived at the city gates, still singing praises, Pharisees were standing by scowling and saying, "Do you see how you prevail nothing? You can't stop him. The whole world has gone after him."

The Pharisees realized that nothing they were doing was keeping the people from following Jesus and calling him the Messiah. They feared it would attract the attention of the Romans and bring trouble upon them.

Later, walking back to Bethany, still rejoicing and recounting the events of the day, Father said anxiously, "I'm afraid- very afraid – of what lies ahead."

Chapter 17

A CONFESSION

Tobias woke before daybreak, too excited to go back to sleep. Being careful not to wake his cousins, he rolled up his sleeping mat and laid it alongside a wall. He picked up his sandals and walked barefooted toward the sounds of men's voices coming from the main part of the house. Eager to hear what they were saying, he paused only long enough to grab a chunk of day old bread.

Tobias moved quietly toward the men, hoping that in the dimness of early dawn he would not be noticed. But then he remembered! It didn't matter now. He was a man! He was now one of them.

The voices he heard were not only those of his relatives. Had no one slept last night? Small clusters of men gathered in the courtyard and alongside the path in front of Uncle Abe's house. Some were talking softly; others nearly shouting. Tobias could almost taste the excitement in the air as he moved among them catching snatches of conversations.

"If Jesus is the Messiah, He's the deliverer sent by God to deliver us from our enemies," said one.

"How will He deliver us? How will He do it?" questioned another.

"The Messiah is God's instrument promised in the Scriptures. He's the head of the Armies of Heaven," shouted a learned man.

A Confession

"Maybe He will call down a company of angels!" called out one of the younger men.

"The scriptures say the Messiah comes as Judge of the Nations," a neighbor suggested in a quiet voice. "He is the ruler of the Kingdom. Jesus has already shown us his power."

"But what will He do now? Will He build an army to defeat the Romans?" broke in Uncle Abe.

"No," responded a neighbor. "The Pharisees teach that the Messiah will appear in God's good time, and that through Him the law will be fulfilled."

"True. But the Zealots believe the Messiah will bring national deliverance by force," another called out in a loud voice.

"Some say that deliverance will come in the Day of the Lord after a horrible conflict."

By the time Tobias had heard all the opinions, his brain was swirling. *Who was right? Would Jesus build up an army of men and angels and wage war against the Romans?*

Tobias went apart from the men. All these ideas about what Jesus would do confused him. Tobias shook his head as if to clear his mind and tried to remember all that Jesus said about himself.

He said He was the good shepherd, that He came not to be ministered to, but to minister. He even said that He came to give His life as a ransom for many. He taught about loving your neighbor, about mercy and forgiveness, and humility. None of those things sounded warlike!

Tobias' thoughts were interrupted by his Father's voice, calling, "Tobias, where are you? Come now. We must go into Jerusalem to deliver linen to Joseph of Arimathea."

The market place was thronged with people who had come to Jerusalem for the Passover: merchants, buyers and sellers, and, here, too, small groups of men talking and shouting. Tobias and his father strolled among them looking

The Hour Is Now

for Joseph of Arimathea.

When Father caught a glimpse of the wealthy man talking with a small group of merchants, he nudged Tobias saying, "Come along. There's Joseph now."

As they approached the very important man, Father said, "Be careful what you say, Tobias, Joseph is a counselor, a member of the Sanhedrin."

As they drew near, Joseph looked up, saw them, and stepped away from the men to greet them.

"Ah, there you are my friend! I can't wait to see the linen you bring. Your work is so fine." Then he chuckled. "It's expensive, but well worth the cost!"

Joseph folded back a corner of the wrapping to examine the fabric. Well pleased, he opened the leather pouch of shekels hanging at his waist to pay for the fine white linen.

"So, my friend," Joseph said, "I suppose you've heard the many rumors about this man, Jesus."

Hesitating for only a second, Father replied, "Yes, I have heard."

"I understand he comes from Capernaum. Do you know him, or his followers?"

"Capernaum is a small fishing village, Joseph. It would be hard not to know everyone there."

Joseph smiled. "I know, I know. Let me put it another way. Do *you* follow his teachings?"

This time, there was no hesitation. Tobias was proud when his father responded, "I do, Joseph. We have heard His teachings and seen His miracles. In fact, my son Tobias, here, has experienced one. His lame foot was healed by Jesus. I not only believe His teachings. I believe Jesus is the Messiah."

Joseph gazed at Tobias and said, "My boy, how blessed you are to have been touched by the very Son of God!" Then Joseph laid a hand on Father's shoulder and squeezed it gently. "You see, I, too, believe Jesus is the Messiah. But as a member of the council, the Sanhedrin, I must be careful of what I say and do. Many seek to destroy Jesus. I trust you, and I'm glad that we share a belief in Jesus."

"And I trust you, Joseph. These are dangerous times. I fear for Jesus – and for his followers."

"I, too, am afraid that things will only get worse," said Joseph." Be careful, friend – and keep the faith."

As they returned to Bethany, Tobias asked, "Father, did you forget your warning to be careful about what we said to Joseph of Arimathea?"

"No, my son, I didn't forget. But I cannot deny the One who gave my heart eyes to see truth; no matter what it may cost me."

Chapter 18

AN ANOINTING

Great crowds of people followed Jesus from Mount Olivet to Jerusalem where Jesus taught daily in the temple. Scribes and Pharisees continued to try to trick him with questions, but his followers were delighted with how Jesus fielded the questions with parables.

Jesus' enemies knew the parables were often about them and their anger grew. They plotted and schemed how they might destroy Jesus, but they were afraid of the people, especially during these feast days.

Wandering the streets of Bethany, Tobias sensed expectancy among the people. When would Jesus make his move? Would He build an army? If so, how would He do it?

Tobias also heard impatience in men's voices. Why did Jesus continue to teach about love and humility when He had come to deliver them from Roman rule? Why wasn't He stirring up the people to fight? What was He waiting for?

Then Tobias remembered Jesus' words: "My time has not come." Was Jesus waiting for the right time – His time?

Shortly after mid-day Uncle Abe came into the house where the women were sweeping and cleaning to get rid of any leaven in preparation for Passover. "Be sure you find

An Anointing

every speck," he admonished before leaving again to look for Father and Grandfather.

Tobias followed his uncle to the courtyard where Father and Grandfather were talking and he heard Abe say, "I just learned that Simon, one of the lepers Jesus healed, is hosting a banquet this evening. He lives here in Bethany. And Jesus will be at the banquet. Perhaps we'll learn of His plans."

"Have we been invited?" asked Father.

"It's an informal banquet, and even though we aren't seated, we'll be able to see and hear everything from the street."

Tobias was excited by the thought of seeing Jesus and perhaps hearing his plans. The afternoon passed slowly, so slowly: would it never be time to walk to Simon's house?

When they arrived at the courtyard of Simon's house, they saw tables arranged in a U shape with an opening at one end for servants to enter to serve the guests. Sloping couches had been placed around the sides of the tables. Curtains separated the dining area from the street in such a way that passersby could look in to observe the banquet.

Tobias saw men on every couch. Not only were the disciples and some of Jesus' followers lounging alongside the tables, there were also scribes and Pharisees; known enemies of Jesus. *What were they doing here*? Tobias wondered.

Father had the same question. "Why are those who hate Jesus here?" he asked Abe. "I doubt that Simon invited them! I suppose he couldn't very well refuse them hospitality. Still ..."

Servants brought platters of meats, bread, fruits, and cheese to place before the men. Lying on their sides on the couches, leaning on one arm with feet and legs behind them, the guests could easily reach the food with the other arm while talking with one another.

Goblets of wine were refilled often as Simon played the perfect host. Guests laughed and talked among themselves, although the scribes and Pharisees did not seem to be enjoying themselves. Most wore scowls as they listened to the conversations and observed the attention given to Jesus.

As the banquet was drawing to a close, the curtains parted and a woman stepped through to approach the tables! Men gasped. No! This couldn't be! Women never dared enter a men's gathering.

But this woman did.

Not only that, her unloosed hair swung freely down her back. Virtuous women kept their hair covered. Only a woman of ill repute would uncover her hair before men other than her own family.

Walking gracefully, carrying a beautiful alabaster jar, the woman moved toward where Jesus was reclining. Jesus smiled at her. Returning the smile, she stepped closer to Jesus. Then to the amazement of the guests, she broke the jar to pour its contents, expensive spikenard, on Jesus' head. The fragrance floated on the air, reaching even the men on the street.

Some of the guests, even one of the disciples, muttered, "Why did she waste this ointment? It might have been sold and the money given to the poor."

But Jesus said, "Let her alone. Why do you trouble her? You will have the poor among you always, but you will not always have me. She has done a good work. She has come to anoint my body for burying."

"Anoint Jesus for burying!" Tobias blurted. What was Jesus saying? Even the disciples looked confused.

Now the scribes and Pharisees began whispering to one another. Tobias watched Judas Iscariot stand to leave the banqueting table. He had a strange expression on his face. Tobias thought it looked as if he were sneaking away.

When the woman moved as quietly as she came to leave through the parted curtains, everyone knew the banquet was over. Guests began to drift away from Simon's house.

Street watchers wandered off. A few were shaking their heads in bewilderment; including Tobias, Father, Uncle Abe, and Grandfather.

CHAPTER 19

A SACRIFICE

Tobias was still thinking about all that had taken place the night before at Simon's house when Uncle Abe approached him saying, "Tobias, today I must take the lamb for our Passover feast to the Temple to be blessed and slaughtered. Would you like to go with me?"

"Yes, Uncle Abe. I'll be happy to go and to see more of the Temple," Tobias responded.

The lamb that Uncle Abe selected from his small flock was pure white with not a spot or blemish. Tobias thought he had never seen so perfect a lamb. It looked so trusting and innocent Tobias felt almost sad that it had to be killed.

When they arrived in Jerusalem, the sun glistened on the white marble of Herod's Temple. Gold decorations gleamed, dazzling Tobias' eyes. Even though the Temple was not yet finished, Tobias had never seen anything so beautiful.

"We will enter the Temple area from the north through the Sheep Gate, Tobias, and then go to where the animals are slain before we go to the Court of Priests to have the sacrifice blessed."

Passing through the Sheep Gate, Uncle Abe said, "Look, Over there, Tobias", as he pointed to a large rectangular pool with five porches. "That is the Pool of Bethesda."

"Why are all those people laying around the pool?" asked Tobias.

"They are invalids, too ill to walk or care for themselves. They're waiting for an angel to stir the water. They believe that if someone will place them in the pool after the angel has troubled the water, they will be healed. Tobias, have you not heard what Jesus did not long ago at this pool?"

"No. Please tell me, Uncle Abe."

"When Jesus was in the Temple area one Sabbath day, he came by the pool and saw a man that had been waiting for thirty-eight years to be put in the water. Jesus asked him, 'Wilt thou be made whole?' The man said, 'I have no one to put me in the water. While I wait another always steps in before me.'"

"Did Jesus help him into the water?" asked Tobias.

"No," laughed Uncle Abe. "He did better than that! He said, 'Rise, take up your bed and walk.' And the man immediately was made whole." Uncle Abe paused a moment and then went on, saying, "The problem is, once again it was the Sabbath and the priests and other authorities were furious. They were not only angry that Jesus healed on the Sabbath, they were furious that so many people were following Jesus. They were afraid that his followers would no longer listen to them and obey their rules. They began to accuse Jesus of breaking the Sabbath rules."

"What did Jesus say?"

"He said something that made them even angrier. He said, 'Man was not made for the Sabbath; the Sabbath was made for man.' He also said, once again, that the Son of Man was Lord of the Sabbath."

"Oh, Uncle Abe, what do you think the authorities will do to Jesus?"

"I don't know, Tobias. I do know that there are plots to get rid of him. I heard they have even sent out spies to watch every move Jesus makes. He is in great danger."

As they waited for their turn to have the lamb slaughtered, Uncle Abe asked, "Did anyone ever tell you that when John the Baptist was baptizing at the Jordan River, he saw Jesus approaching and said, 'Behold, the Lamb of God that takes away the sins of the world'?"

"Yes, I did hear that, but I didn't really understand, Uncle Abe. The Torah teaches that there must be a blood sacrifice for sin. That's why we offer animal sacrifices, to make an offering for our sins. I wonder how John thought that Jesus could take away the sin of the whole world."

"I don't completely understand, either, Tobias. I'm beginning to think there are many mysteries surrounding Jesus that will only be revealed to us in time. Now we must take the sacrifice to the priest to be blessed. Then we can start back home."

After the sacrificial part of the lamb had been blessed, Uncle Abe was given the part they were to take home to be roasted and eaten. No less than ten men by law and custom, and as many as twenty would eat of this one lamb.

As they walked home, carrying the portion of lamb that would be eaten the following day at their Passover meal, Tobias thought again about something Uncle Abe had said earlier, "In time the mysteries will be revealed."

There it was again; in time. Jesus said His time has not yet come. What did He mean by His time? What mysteries might be revealed when His time came? Tobias wondered.

Chapter 20

A MEAL

Smoke drifted into the house, carrying with it the mouth watering odors of lamb seasoned with spices roasting over the open spit in the courtyard. Bustling sounds and the smell of baking bread filled the house. Tobias peeked into the cooking area to see busy women preparing food for the Passover Feast.

It was a special day – a happy day – and for Tobias an important day. This was the first year that he was old enough to be counted as one of the required ten men to eat the Passover meal.

By late afternoon, the roasted lamb was ready to be eaten. Cushions for the men lined three sides of a long table covered with a snowy white cloth that Tobias recognized as one of his mother's weavings. Wineskins and cups marked the head of the table where Uncle Abe would recline.

A platter of lamb held the place of honor in the center of the table. Bowls of bitter herbs, apples, and sweet sauces dotted the white linen. Baskets of unleavened bread stood ready for dipping in sweet sauce.

The men arranged themselves on the cushions around the table; the food was in place. The meal could begin.

Uncle Abe, as the head of the family, poured a cup of wine, held it up and blessed it before passing it for all to drink. Then Tobias' cousin, Uncle Abe's eldest son, asked the traditional question, "What is the meaning of the feast?"

Tobias never tired of hearing the story of Moses leading the Hebrews out of slavery in Egypt. This day the story seemed even more exciting as Uncle Abe recounted the story of the Exodus. He thrilled to the part where God told Moses the Hebrew families were to kill a lamb and put its blood on the lintel and sides of the doorway of their homes so the angel of death would pass over. From that day on, the Passover feast would celebrate the Hebrew children's delivery from slavery.

Tobias raised his voice to sing the Hallel, psalms of praise, with the others, glad that he had learned the Psalms in synagogue school, even though his voice now sometimes cracked on the high notes. The second cup of wine was blessed and passed. Then the men could begin eating.

The savory lamb reminded the men of the sacrifice that had been made to obtain blood for the Hebrews to place on their doorposts. Bitter herbs on the table reminded them of the bitterness of slavery in Egypt. Unleavened cakes dipped in sweet sauce spoke of the sweetness of escape and of the manna God provided when the Israelites wandered in the wilderness. Unleavened bread reminded them of the haste with which the Hebrew people had to be ready to leave. There was no time to waste waiting for dough to rise!

Then a prayer of thanksgiving was offered.

The third cup was blessed and passed and, during the passing of the fourth cup, more Psalms were sung.

After the meal was finished, the men relaxed around the table. Now talk turned once again to Jesus.

Tobias listened quietly. He wondered where Jesus was celebrating the Passover. *Was He, too, even now singing the Hallel?*

Chapter 21

AN ARREST

"He's been taken! They've stolen Him away." The words shouted at an alarming pitch broke into Tobias' half dreams.

"Who's been taken?" he heard his Grandfather call out. "What's all the shouting about?"

"Jesus!" shouted another voice. "They've taken Jesus! The soldiers came into the garden where Jesus and some of the disciples were praying and they arrested Him."

"What do you mean arrested Him? Who arrested him? And why would they arrest Jesus? Surely there's no law against praying!" a woman's voice cried out.

The commotion had by now drawn a crowd of anxious people.

"I heard that the authorities have accused Him of blasphemy and of stirring up a riot," said an elderly man in a shaky voice.

"That's a pack of lies," said Father. "Besides, they can't accuse Jesus of blasphemy without witnesses."

"But they say they have witnesses," said a man who had just joined the crowd. "They are false witnesses that the chief priests, scribes, and elders paid to give false witness, but witnesses all the same."

"How did they know where to find the Master?" a young woman cried out.

An Arrest

"I was told that Judas Iscariot led the group of soldiers when they entered the Garden at Gethsemene. Apparently he went up to Jesus, said, 'Hail, Master', kissed Him on the cheek, and in that way identified Him to the soldiers."

"Judas!" shouted several men. "Why would he betray Jesus? He is one of the Messiah's followers!"

"Yes, but he is also a Zealot. He expected Jesus to incite a revolt against Rome. It's rumored that Judas was even paid thirty pieces of silver to betray Jesus."

A dark silence fell upon the crowd.

Tobias remembered the angry expression on Judas' face at the banquet at Simon's house and how he seemed to leave secretly.

Betrayal.
   Lies.
      Treachery.

Jesus, who taught only love and forgiveness, handed over to his enemies for no just reason. Jesus, betrayed by one of his disciples.

"Did none of the disciples try to stop the soldiers?" demanded one of the men.

"They say that Peter drew his sword and cut off the ear of one of them, but Jesus told Peter to put his sword away. After that, the rest of the disciples fled and the soldiers took Jesus away."

Tobias' voice pierced the silence. "Where have they taken Jesus?"

"They took him to the house of Caiaphas, the high priest, Annas' son-in-law, to be judged by the council," spoke a latecomer.

"Come on!" Tobias shouted. "We have to go quickly. We have to tell the council that these are all lies!"

Tobias began running along the path from Bethany to Jerusalem; soon others – men and women, - joined him.

There was no time to lose. The slap of Tobias' sandals on the path kept pace with the thumping of his heart. Hurry – hurry – hurry.

But they were too late.

When they reached the house of the high priest, the courtyard was empty except for a few men. They saw none of the chief priests, elders or scribes. Nor were the disciples anywhere to be found. One of the men said he thought he had seen Peter earlier, sitting by a fire in the courtyard speaking to a maidservant.

He went on to say that the council had asked for witnesses against Jesus to put him to death. But no one came forth until some false witnesses were called. And they couldn't agree with each other.

"But that's illegal!" Grandfather said. "According to authorities' own laws, trials may not be held in darkness."

"What did they do then?" Father asked grimly.

Another man replied, "That's when the high priest stood and asked Jesus, 'So do you not answer? What is it that these witness against you?' But Jesus said nothing.

Then the high priest asked, 'Art thou the Christ, the Son of the Blessed?'"

Tobias felt his father's grip on his shoulder tighten when his father asked, "And what did Jesus answer?"

After a moment's hesitation, the first man replied, "Jesus said, 'I AM, and you will see the Son of Man sitting on the right hand of power and come in the clouds of heaven.'"

One of the women listening moaned, "Oh, no. They trapped him!"

"Yes," the man continued." As soon as the council members heard Jesus say, 'I AM', they started shouting. The high priest said, 'You have heard the blasphemy. We need no further witnesses.'

And they condemned Jesus to die. Other council members spat on him and blindfolded him. Some struck him and mocked him saying, 'Prophesy.' When dawn broke they took him to Pilate to be judged."

"To be judged by Pilate!" Father said. "Let's make haste!"

Chapter 22

A Trial

But again they were too late.

When they reached Pilate's house, the courtyard was beginning to fill with people looking for excitement. Members of the Sanhedrin moved among them, stirring up anger. Pressing through the gathering crowd, the small band of followers made a way to the porch just as Pilate stepped out from his inner chamber. They heard his voice saying, "I find in him no fault at all. But you have a custom that I should release a prisoner to you at Passover. Shall I release to you the King of the Jews?"

But the crowd shouted, "We have no king, but Caesar! Release not this man, but give us the robber Barabbas!"

Pilate turned on his heel and went back into his house. When he came out a second time, he was not alone. Jesus was with him. Gesturing toward Jesus, Pilate said, "I bring this man forth to you so that you may know that I find no fault in him."

As Jesus stepped forward, Pilate pointed to him and shouted, "Behold the Man!"

Those who loved Jesus gasped in horror. They barely recognized the Master. His marred face was bruised and badly beaten. A purple robe had been thrown around his shoulders. A crown of thorns pressed upon his head pierced his skin; blood from the thorns' wounds streamed down his cheeks, matting his beard.

Again Pilate spoke. "I have scourged him. You see what

The Hour Is Now

Herod's soldiers have done to your king. Is this not punishment enough?"

But when the chief priests and officers saw Jesus, they cried out, "Crucify him! Crucify him!"

Tobias' voice cried out, "No! No! Let the Messiah go!" But it was lost in the tumult.

The sixth hour drew near and Pilate called out, "Shall I crucify your king?"

"Do away with him! Give us Barabbas," shouted the officers. "Barabbas! Barabbas!"

Pilate called for a bowl of water. Dipping into the water, he said, "I am innocent of the blood of this just person. I wash my hands of it. You see to it."

"Let his blood be on us and on our children," the mob cried.

So Pilate released Barabbas and delivered Jesus to them to be crucified.

The soldiers stripped the robe from Jesus, struck him with their hands and mocked him, saying, "Hail, King of the Jews!" Tobias, seeing the bleeding stripes on Jesus' back from the scourging, cried out, "It's not fair! He's done nothing wrong! You can't do this to Him!

The soldiers hit Jesus with a reed - and spit upon him - and knelt before him in mockery, pretending to worship. Then they put his own clothes back on him to take him out to crucify him.

Tobias felt the crushing weight when the soldiers laid a heavy wooden cross on Jesus' shoulders. As they began to lead him away, Tobias moaned, "Father, where are they taking Him?"

"To Golgotha; the place of the skull," Father answered. "Where He'll be crucified like a common thief," he added bitterly. "Come, Tobias, we will go back to Uncle Abe's."

"No, Father," Tobias said. "I can't leave Jesus now. I want to be with Him."

"No, Tobias," Father protested, knowing what lay ahead for Jesus. "It's too much – you mustn't stay …

"Yes, Father, I must stay with Jesus," insisted Tobias.

Chapter 23

A Crucifixion

Broken hearted, Tobias, Father and Grandfather joined others, some of them women, to walk alongside Jesus on the dusty winding path leading to Golgotha. Weak from the beatings and loss of blood, Jesus staggered under the weight of the cross

"Help Him!" Tobias cried out. "Please won't someone help?" Finally one of the soldiers seized a man named Simon who was from Cyrene and forced him to help carry the cross.

As they neared the hill of Golgotha, two crosses, each bearing a crucified thief, stood outlined against the reddening morning sky. Soldiers waited on the hillside for the next victim.

The little group of followers drew close enough to see the arresting soldiers shove Jesus forward. Other soldiers grabbed him roughly by the shoulders and forced him to the ground.

Tobias, thankfully, could not see the soldiers position Jesus with outstretched arms on the cross. But he was near enough to hear the ring of the hammer as nails were driven through Jesus' wrists and feet. Each blow of the hammer tore through Tobias' heart.

When the cross bearing Jesus was lifted in place between the two thieves, Tobias saw that a crude sign bearing the words JESUS OF NAZARETH KING OF THE JEWS had been nailed above Jesus' head.

What had happened? How could it be, that Jesus, the Son of God, the Messiah, was crucified on a cross of shame? A ball of rage and disappointment choked Tobias' throat.

When the soldiers began casting lots for Jesus' cloak at the foot of the cross, Father's voice rang out. "You're nothing but pigs!" he shouted.

At that moment Jesus looked down from the cross at the people below. Tobias saw the sorrow in Jesus' eyes when He said, "Father, forgive them; they know not what they do."

Forgive them? Jesus was praying for God to forgive His enemies? It was too much for Tobias. Maybe God could forgive such treachery, but he, Tobias, would not.

The group of onlookers began to break up. As they passed by the foot of Jesus' cross, many wagged their heads and taunted him saying. "If you are the son of God, come down from the cross." "King of the Jews, are you?" they sneered. One of the chief priests scoffed, "He saved others, but cannot save himself!"

Even one of the thieves said, "If you be the Christ, save yourself and us."

But the other thief said, "Do you not fear God seeing you also are condemned? We receive what we deserve for what we have done, but this man has done nothing wrong." Then turning his head toward Jesus, he said, "Remember me when you come into your Kingdom."

Jesus said to him, "Truly, I say unto you. Today you will be with me in paradise."

Immediately the sun disappeared. Darkness covered the earth. Those standing near heard Jesus cry out, "My God, my God, why have you forsaken me?"

Now only a few people remained. The excitement of another crucifixion was nearly over.

Tobias saw Mary and several other women at the foot of the cross weeping as they gazed up at Jesus. The disciple, John, stood nearby.

Jesus lifted his head to nod toward John saying, "Mother, behold your son." Then he spoke to John. "Behold your

A Crucifixion

mother." John drew close to Mary to comfort her as Jesus' head dropped again to one side.

Finally Jesus said, "I thirst." There was a vessel of vinegar close by. The soldiers dipped a sponge into the vinegar, put the sponge on hyssop, and brought it to Jesus' mouth. When Jesus had received the vinegar, he said, "It is finished. Father, into thy hands I commend my spirit."

The earth shuddered; rocks split in two. A terrified centurion cried out, "Surely this was the Son of God!"

Sobbing, struggling to hold back unmanly tears, Tobias saw soldiers approach with staves in their hands. "Now what are they doing? Surely there's nothing more they can do to Him!"

Grandfather said, "Because it grows late and the bodies cannot remain on the cross on the Sabbath, the Jews must have asked Pilate to have their legs broken so that death will come and the bodies can be taken down."

"But Grandfather," Tobias began to say ...

"I know, I know, son. There is no need to break the Messiah's legs. Jesus' spirit has departed. He has gone from us."

The soldiers broke the legs of the two thieves to hasten their deaths. When they realized that Jesus was already dead, they didn't break His legs, but one of the soldiers thrust a spear into His side. Blood and water burst forth.

Immediately Tobias thought of the lamb slaughtered for the Passover and he remembered once more the words of John the Baptist. "Behold the Lamb of God who takes away the sins of the world."

Lambs were offered as a sacrifice for sin; their blood poured out. Now Jesus' blood had been spilled. Tobias clutched Uncle Abe's arm. "Uncle Abe, the prophet's words, 'He gave his life as a ransom ...' Is this part of the mystery we talked about? Did Jesus, God's own son, the Lamb of God, give His life for us, for our sins?"

Tobias spun around to face his grandfather. "Why, Grandfather? Why did Jesus have to die?"

Father put his arm around Tobias' shoulders, saying,

"Come, son. We must go. There's nothing to be done. It's all over now."

Later that black day, news from Jerusalem began to spread throughout Bethany.

"Some say that just before He died, when Jesus said, 'Father, into thy hands I commend my spirit,' the veil in the temple ripped down the middle from the top to the bottom!"

"Did you know that Joseph of Arimathea asked Pilate for the body of Jesus so that he might bury it? He brought beautiful white linen to wrap the body for burial."

"Nicodemus brought about a hundred pound weight of myrrh and aloes to prepare Jesus' body for burial."

"They placed the body in Joseph's own tomb."

"The officials were so afraid that someone would steal the body they rolled a huge stone across the opening."

Tobias couldn't bear to hear any more. Nothing else mattered now. Jesus, his teacher, the One he loved so much, the One who had healed him, was gone.

The Messiah was dead.

They killed Him.

Chapter 24

A RESURRECTION

The Sabbath day at Uncle Abe's passed slowly. After a sleepless night filled with horrible dreams, Tobias was glad when morning came. Soon they would be leaving for home. Maybe, back in Capernaum, he could begin to forget the terrible events of attending his first Passover in Jerusalem.

Later that morning a loud knocking at the door startled the family. "What next?" Uncle Abe muttered. "Nothing can be so important at this point."

When the door swung open, an excited neighbor burst through shouting, "He's alive! He's alive!"

"Who is alive? What are you talking about, man?"

"Jesus! Jesus is alive!"

"Stop talking foolishness. Jesus was crucified and buried. You've spent too much time at the wineskin!"

"No, you don't understand. I'm not drunk. Well, maybe I am – drunk with joy. They couldn't kill him! Jesus has risen from the dead!"

By this time the entire family had gathered to hear the neighbor's raving. "What do you mean, risen from the dead?" asked Grandfather.

"I mean just what I said." The words tumbled out. "Mary Magdalene went to the garden tomb early this morning with spices to anoint Jesus' body. She saw that the stone had been rolled away. Mary looked in and the tomb was empty. She ran to tell Simon Peter and John that the body had been taken."

"Empty?" said Father. "Who took his body away?"

"No one took him away! His burial clothes were lying in the tomb, but Jesus was gone. Peter and John raced to the tomb. They looked in and also saw that the tomb was empty and the linen clothes were still in the tomb. Then they believed Mary and went to tell the others."

"Well, someone must have stolen the body away," said Father.

"No, no. That's just it. There's more," the man went on. "After Peter and John left, Mary began to cry. She bent to look again into the cave and saw two angels; one at the head and the other at the foot of where Jesus had lain."

"Angels!" said Grandfather. "Mary Magdalene saw angels?"

"Yes! The angels asked why she was weeping. She told them that it was because someone had taken Jesus away. Then, when she turned back from the tomb, she saw Jesus standing there! But she didn't know it was Jesus."

Now the family was dumbfounded. The tomb was empty? Angels? And then Jesus himself appears!

"How did she come to realize it was Jesus?" asked Uncle Abe.

"Jesus also asked why she was weeping and asked whom she was seeking. When she told Him, thinking he was the gardener, and asked where he had taken the body, Jesus said, 'Mary'. The minute she heard him speak her name, she recognized Him. She fell at his feet, and said, 'Master.' Jesus told her to go to his brethren and tell them that He would ascend to His Father, to His God and their God."

"Are you sure of all this?" asked Father.

"Yes! Yes, I'm sure! And that's not all. Later in the day Jesus appeared to the disciples themselves. They saw the nail prints in His hands and feet. It's true, I tell you! Jesus the Christ arose from the dead. He's alive!"

A Resurrection

In the beginning, it seemed impossible to believe; that Jesus their Messiah was indeed alive! But stories abounded of many people who had seen the risen Jesus and the good news spread. Jesus, the Messiah, had been crucified. He died, was dead and buried, but He rose from the dead and was alive!

Alive! Tobias wanted to run through the streets shouting, "Alive! Jesus is alive!"

And so he did, telling everyone he met the Good News. Jesus the Christ, the Messiah, rose from the dead!

After that many more people saw Jesus. Every day many more believed that Jesus was truly the Messiah sent by God.

Tobias thought again and again of John the Baptist's words. "Behold the Lamb of God who comes to take away the sins of the world."

Now, at last, Tobias understood. Jesus came, not to save the people from the Romans, but to save them from their own sin. He didn't have to die! God's own Son could have called ten thousand angels to protect Him. He sacrificed himself so they could be forgiven. He paid the ransom for sin. He died to save Tobias from *his* sin; including the sin of being unwilling to forgive.

"Jesus the Christ, God's own Son, the Messiah gave His life for me, Tobias thought. The tears Tobias had struggled so hard to hold back streaked his dusty cheeks. Now they were tears of joy.

Jesus spent forty days with his disciples teaching them what they needed to know to carry on the work of the Kingdom. Toward the end of the forty days, Jesus told them that He must return to His Father, but that He would not leave them comfortless. He said He would send His Spirit to be with them and to teach them all things. He told the disciples

The Hour Is Now

to go to Jerusalem and wait for the gift of His Spirit.

Ten days later, the disciples and 120 other followers met together in Jerusalem to pray and wait. Suddenly, as they prayed, a sound like a mighty rushing wind filled the house where they were staying. Tongues of fire fell on each of them; the promised gift of the Holy Spirit had come!

The disciples began speaking and praising God in languages they had never learned. People who had come to Jerusalem from many different countries heard the disciples speaking in their own languages. At first they thought the disciples were drunk! But Peter told them they were not drunk, but filled with the Holy Spirit, just as the prophet Joel said they would be. That day 3000 were added to the number of believers in Jesus.

The gift of the Holy Spirit gave the disciples power to preach and carry out Jesus' command to take the Good News to all corners of the earth. Many signs and wonders were done by the disciples. Believers were added to the company every day as they continued to meet together for breaking bread from house to house.

For Tobias, the best Good News of all was hearing the disciples tell of seeing Jesus ascend into heaven in a cloud and the wonderful, incredible news that Jesus would come back again the same way that He ascended. And when that time came, they said, the whole world would see him come! His Kingdom would come; His will would be done on earth as it was in heaven.

Even though Jesus was gone away, Tobias felt closer to Him than ever. As He promised, He wouldn't leave them alone. His Spirit would always be with them.

But, oh, how Tobias longed for His return.

Epilogue

A BEGINNING

Sixteen year old Tobias returned home from delivering fabric. He loved working alongside his father, but even more he loved talking about Jesus to his customers, risky though it was. A risk he and his family were willing to take to serve Jesus. Miriam often wove a tiny fish, the secret symbol of Christ followers, on the corner of each bolt of cloth, to identify them as People of the Way.

Tobias entered his home to let his family know that Jonas' father had been arrested for his faith in Jesus and that they must pray for his release. Tomorrow's gathering of the believers could not now be at the nobleman's house.

At least, thought Tobias, *Jonas' father is still alive, not like Stephen who, a year ago, had been stoned to death for preaching about Jesus.*

Tobias found the house to be unusually quiet. No bustling sounds of activity greeted him. Glancing around the room, he saw Rachel sitting in a corner, eyes down cast, hands folded.

Miriam came to meet him, her face stained with tears, saying, "Go to your Grandfather, Tobias. He's waiting for you."

Tobias moved on silent feet to where his beloved Grandfather lay in the sleeping quarter.

"Come closer, grandson," Grandfather whispered, reaching out to take Tobias' hand in his own. "We've had quite a time together, haven't we?"

"Yes, grandfather. We've had wonderful times ... as well as some hard ones."

"True," Grandfather agreed. "With more hard times to come, I fear. Now it's time for me to move on."

"No, Grandfather, no ..." Tobias started to say.

Grandfather gently squeezed Tobias' hand. "It's the way it's meant to be, lad. You mustn't feel sadness. Don't you remember the Master telling us, 'In my Father's house are many mansions?'" Grandfather smiled, "I'm ready to go to the one He has prepared for me, my boy.

I know you don't want me to leave you. But this is not a parting forever, Tobias. In a little while, I will be with Jesus. Then someday – when the time is right – you and I will be together again – with Him forever. Until then, Tobias, follow Jesus wherever He leads you."

"I will, Grandfather. I'll go wherever He sends me and do whatever He asks me to do. I love Him, and I love you, Grandfather."

"I know you do. No more than I love you, Tobias." Grandfather pressed Tobias' hand to his own lips, then smiled as he said, "I remember how, when you were a little boy, you liked to listen to my stories. You never wanted them to end! Of course, they had to end, but our story *has* no end, grandson. It's really only just ...

The Beginning.
Jesus' time has come.
The Hour Is Now

Events in the Life of Jesus as related in **The Hour Is Now** with a Scripture Reference

The Wedding in Cana	John 2:1–12
Cleansing of the Temple	John 2:13-25
Woman at the Well	John 14:14-42
Healing of Nobleman's Son	John 4:46-54
Blessing the Children	Mark 10:13-16
Teaching in Parables	Luke 8:4-15
Feeding the Multitude	John 6:1-13
Walking on Water	John 6:15-21
Healing a Palsied Man	Mark 2:1-7
Breaking a Sabbath Rule	Matthew 12:1-8
Healing a Withered Hand	Matthew 12:9-14
Healing a Blind Man	John 9:1-25
Raising Lazarus	John 11:1-46
Palm Sunday	John 12:12-19
Anointing at Banquet	John 12:1-8
Healing at Pool of Bethesda	John 5:1-9
The Arrest	John 18:1-14
The Trial	John 18:25-19:1-16
The Crucifixion	John 19:23-42
The Resurrection	John 20:1-18
The Ascension	Luke 24:50-53
The Transfiguration	Matthew 17:1-8

www.ingramcontent.com/pod-product-compliance
Ingram Content Group UK Ltd.
Pitfield, Milton Keynes, MK11 3LW, UK
UKHW022222230426
12048UKWH00016BA/1012